Operation
Soviet
Union

Johannes Reimer

Logos Biblical Training by Extension

and

Gospel Literature International

July 7, 2000
For Bob Kraus,
with compliments from:

LIGHT IN THE EAST

P.O. Box 1126, Ridgefield, CT. 06877-9126

Sending the Gospel Light to the C.I.S.,
Baltics & Eastern Europe since 1920

Operation Soviet Union:
How to Pray for the 160 People Groups in the USSR

- Information
- Background
- Opportunities

Johannes Reimer

LOGOS Biblical Training by Extension
and
Gospel Literature International

LOGOS
P.O. Box 409
Fresno, CA
93708-0409

GLINT USA
Box 488
Rosemead, CA 91770

GLINT CANADA
1300 Bloor St., #1708
Mississauga, Ont.
L4X3Z2 Canada

LOGOS
P.O. Box 409
Fresno, CA
93708-0409

GLINT USA
Box 488
Rosemead, CA 91770

GLINT CANADA
1300 Bloor St., #1708
Mississauga, Ont. L4X3Z2
Canada

This work is an English translation of *Gebet für die Völker der Sowjetunion* by Johannes Reimer.

Library of Congress Cataloging-in-Publication Data applied for

To the first missionaries from the Soviet Union who went to the Islamic and Siberian peoples

TABLE OF CONTENTS

Preface to the English Edition

With the advent of Glasnost, it has been a revelation to many in North America to discover the diverse ethnicity of the Soviet Union. In the past, we spoke only of Russians and imagined an entire land of people, European in appearance. More recently, we have had to adjust our perceptions to include Azerbaidzhans, Uzbecks, and Kazaks, just to name a few.

As you read this book you will discover not only a myriad of peoples but cultures and societies with roots in ancient history; Persians, descendants of Genghis Khan, and the relatives of native North Americans. Hidden from our view until now, many of these people have been left out of our prayers and by-passed by mission. Relatively few possess an adequate translation of the Bible in their own language.

Our hope in bringing this book to you is that you will be amazed and inspired as you learn about the diverse peoples of the Soviet Union. We hope that you are inspired to pray for them and for those who work among them.

With the diversity of ethnic groups and languages, we have attempted to standardize the English edition according to Ronald Wixman's *The Peoples of the USSR: An Ethnographic Handbook* (M.E. Sharpe, Inc. Armonk, N.Y., 1984).

Viktor Reimer
July 1990

INTRODUCTION

The Great Commission is clear, we are to "go and make disciples of all nations...." (Matt. 28:19). It is a commission that includes all countries, races, and social classes; it embraces the entire population of the world. No one is excluded. No one is forgotten. This is a global commission of staggering magnitude. How can the Church of Jesus Christ fulfill this commission?

The political and religious world map changed radically after World War II. Between 1945 and 1985, over 100 new nation states have been established. And, since 1985, glasnost and perestroika portends the establishment of more new nations. However, many nations are still under the influence of Communist regimes. Over 1.7 billion people live under the shadow of the hammer and sickle. With the recent changes that have shaken the Communist dominated world, there are now unprecedented opportunities for the proclamation of the Gospel. But, as it stands, most of the people living under Communism have never heard the Gospel.

The Union of the Soviet Socialist Republics (USSR), the birth place of communism, is the largest Communist dominated country. Over 278 million people, representing 160 different people groups, live in the Soviet Union. Lamentably, only a small percentage of these people groups have heard the saving message of Jesus Christ.

The Great Commission of Jesus Christ includes the Communist world. We must consider the many people groups within the Soviet Union as embraced by Jesus when he said: "And this gospel of the kingdom will be preached in the whole world as a testimony to all nations" (Matt. 24:14).

Most Communist countries have not allowed the church to be active in mission and evangelism. Even with the recent changes in Eastern Europe, it is uncertain of the freedom that is or will be allowed. Even so, if the various countries and states do not grant the freedom to missionize and evangelize, are Christians thereby exempt from taking the Great Commission seriously? It should be remembered that many believers have already given up their freedom, even their lives, for the sake of Christ's mission in the world. Is this price too high in view of eternity? The Great Commission cannot be rescinded through restrictions, persecution, or even fear. It has been and continues to be the life foundation of Christ's church in the East and the West.

Jesus Christ intended to reach the world with his healing message. He did not think this was impossible. Should we? Perhaps it is helpful to reflect on his words once again: "All authority in heaven and on earth is given to me" (Matt. 28:18). Is this authority not sufficient to act against the bastion of Communism?

One of the problems of the church today, as I see it, is its inability to see the world through the eyes of God. This loss of vision places the church in danger of confusing its priorities and of losing its foundation for mission. That is what has happened with regard to the Soviet Union. One sees the terrifying acts of the Communists and hears about the persecution but then forgets the main task — to evangelize the people of this huge country. The Communists need the Word of God also.

13

A correction is needed. I believe this can happen only through personal conversation with God. The Bible testifies that we will be transformed when we speak with Him. Such transformative conversation with God is the aim of this book. The intent is formative, not merely informative. It is designed to assist believers in seeing as God might; to behold the rich harvest field of the hitherto closed country. It is a call to missionize the Soviet Union in participatory prayer.

May the Lord bless the prayers of his children.

I would like to thank all who have helped me write this book: my wife Cornelia who spent many days and hours working at the manuscript, brothers and sisters in the Soviet Union who helped find the information, LOGOS co-workers who wrote some parts, and especially Lydia Schroeder and Helene Tielmann who typed the entire manuscript. I thank all of them.

Above all, I thank the LORD who gave me a vision of mission for my old homeland.

PART I

BACKGROUNDS

1. General Overview

1.1 Land and People

Territorially, the Soviet Union is the largest country in the world and has the third largest population. Within its 22,402,200 square km. live more than 276 million people who represent many races and languages.

Geographically, this gigantic country borders twelve other countries and is surrounded by 12 seas and oceans. The Soviet Union occupies 1/6 of the world's inhabited space; 25% is located in Europe and 75% in Asia. Its length of 11,000 km. crosses 11 time zones and its north-south span is 4,000 km.

Climatic differences in the Soviet Union are staggering; the eternal ice of the north and the sub-tropical climate in the south yield a temperature difference of 120 degrees centigrade. This enormous weather variation provides everything nature lovers might desire: broad steppes and sand deserts, high mountains and the untouched taiga, swamps and lakes, seas and swift rivers. The Russians say that it is a land the earth carries in its heart.

Politically, the Soviet Union (USSR) is a federation of 15 Soviet Republics (SSR) in which more than 130 people groups live. The largest of these groups, the Russians, are actually the lords in the land.

The Soviet Union is a modern industrial state. With industrialization has come urbanization; 62% of the population lives in cities. Twenty-two of these cities have a population of over one million. Growth of cities goes hand in hand with the mobility of the population. In 1977-78 alone, over 20 million people moved. During this migration, people often left their homelands for the first time.

1.2 People Groups and Languages

The Soviet Union has the third largest population in the world. It is nothing less than a multi-nation-state with extreme ethnic and cultural diversity. Of the 91 larger and over 40 smaller people groups, the peoples of the Soviet Union can be divided into ten different language clusters:

a. Slavic People

The Slavic people constitute the largest group within the Soviet Union. In addition to the Russian people (who have the leading role politically, culturally, and economically), the Slavic peoples also include the Ukrainians, Belorussians, Poles, Czechs, Bulgarians, and Slovaks. The last four groups are primarily located in the western parts of the Soviet Union. In contrast, the Russians, Ukrainians, and Belorussians are not only found in their national republics but also in other parts of the Soviet Union.

b. The Baltic People

The Lithuanians and the Latvians constitute the Baltic peoples. The Baltic languages are related to the Slavic languages and probably have the same linguistic roots. Culturally, however, they represent a clearly separate group from the Slavs. The Baltic people settled predominantly in their national republics along the Baltic Sea.

c. The Rumanian People

There are two Rumanian groups represented in the Soviet Union: the Rumanians and the Moldavians. The Moldavians speak a dialect of a Rumanian language which, through the process of Soviet national politics, became a separate language. Most Moldavians and Rumanians live in the Moldavian Soviet Republic or in the border areas in the Ukraine.

d. The Caucasian People

The inhabitants of Caucasus are generally divided into two language groups: the Indo-European and the Non-Indo-European.

The Indo-European Caucasian people includes the Armenians. The Armenians have an ancient culture and have the oldest written language in the Soviet Union.

The Non-Indo-European language family includes the Georgian, Svan, Kabardian, Cherkess, Ingush and Dagestan language groups, and about 40 more smaller people groups.

e. The Turkish People

The Turkish people are the second largest language family in the Soviet Union (following the Slavs) and they are the fastest growing people group. Their settlements reach from the Volga River (Chuvashs, Tatars, and Bashkirs) to the Caucasus Mountains (Azerbaidzhans); from Central Asia (Uzbeks, Kazaks, Turkmen, Karakalpaks, Kirgiz) to Siberia (Tuvins and Yakuts). Their customs and culture were largely influenced by Islam.

f. The Iranian People

The Iranian language family includes the Ossetian people of the Caucasus region and the Tadzhiks of Central Asia.

g. The Finno-Ugrian People

The Finno-Ugrian people belong to the Uralic language family. The settlement of the Finns stretches from the Baltic region (Estonians and Finns) to the Karelic region (Finns and Karelians), from the autonomous Soviet Republics of Komi, Mari, Mordvin, and Udmurt to the Ural mountains. With the exception of the Hungarians in West Ukraine, the Ugric people (Khants and Voguls) live in Northern Siberia.

h. The Mongolian People

This group includes the Kalmucks who live along the Volga's delta and in the steppes of the Caspian Mountains. This language group may be divided into three groups: the Buryats, who live around the Baikal lake in South Siberia; the Sart-Kalpaks, who reside in the Kirgiz SSR; and the Khalkha-Mongolians, who dwell along the border of the Mongolian Republic.

i. The People Groups in Siberia

This language family consists of several small people groups in North Asia who display similarities with the North American Indians. This group includes: the Chukchi; the Koryaks, who live on the Komchatka peninsula; the Gilyaks, who live along the Amur River; the Eskimos; and the Aleutians.

j. Other People Groups

Other people groups came as immigrants and today live in different parts of the Soviet Union. This group includes the Jews, Germans, Greeks, Koreans, Gypsies, Arabs, and Chinese.

1.3 Political and Economic Situation of the People Groups in the Soviet Union

The Union of the Soviet Socialist Republics was founded in 1922 by a federation of four Soviet republics which had existed since the Revolution of 1917. Since that time, the political map has changed many times. Several republics, such as the German Volga Republic, were dissolved. Some were renamed, like the Tadzhik SSR; others were forcefully added, such as the Baltic Republics and Moldavia. In addition, the new government established autonomous areas, counties, or republics for the smaller people groups. Over the course of time, a very complex political structure developed which has the appearance of a multi-nation-state and only occasionally simulates the socialistic dream.

The Soviet Union today consists of 15 Soviet Republics (SSR) which enjoy equal political rights. Some of these republics are divided into Autonomous Soviet Republics (ASSR), Autonomous Counties, and

Autonomous Areas. For example, the Russian Federation (RSFSR) has 16 ASSRs, five Autonomous Counties, and 10 Autonomous Areas. Officially, all of these autonomous areas have a certain political and economic independence; in practice, however, their independence is minimal. Although the diverse people groups have a right to practice their language and culture, they are not allowed, with the exception of the Caucasus Republics, to promote their national languages. That right is exclusively reserved for Russians.

It is true that the Soviet Union, during the past 70 years, has expended some effort in developing the languages of small people groups. Many of the 70 written languages in the modern Soviet Union have been recently developed. This is especially true among the people groups in Siberia and among the nomadic people of Central Asia.

Nevertheless, as a result of these ethnological efforts sponsored by the Soviet Union, a russification of subordinate cultures and languages has occurred. For example, a Cyrillic script was introduced to the already existing Latin script and thus Russian terminology replaced national words, even if it abused the existing language.

Today, the Russian language is not only the trade language in the Soviet Union but also the forced "mother tongue" for the minority groups of this huge country.

Language imposition is only one area which reveals that the Soviet Union is not a socialistic model of a multi-nation-state but a Russian state in Socialist guise.

In order to secure Russian domination, for many years the Soviet state has encouraged a relocation policy aimed at moving Slavic people into the areas of minority groups. In some republics, such as the Baltic Republics, the national population has been shrunk to less than 50%. This is especially evident in urban areas.

Education is another area revealing the russification process. In many autonomous areas, individuals can receive higher education only in Russian. This compels parents to send their children to Russian schools. In this way, minority languages and cultures are lost.

The economic policy has developed in a similar fashion. All national areas, like in the Baltics, receive less economic attention than areas in the RSFSR. Thus, the socialist centralized economy has become an effective tool to control the industrial development of the entire country. Areas which desire stronger national representation are simply ignored. In view of these policies, it is not surprising that one can observe a growing nationalism among the diverse cultural and ethnic groups in the Soviet Union. Needless to say, the Soviet leaders have a difficult time to deal with this unrest. The recent unrest in the Baltic, Caucasus, and Central Asia regions clearly illustrate this growing nationalism.

It is important for Christian missions to remember that a search for national identity is often connected with a search for religious identity. In fact, along with the growing desire for national identity in opposition to Soviet state domination, is the corresponding challenge to the Soviet policy of atheism. Questions about religion and God, therefore, are becoming passionate issues.

1.4 Religious Conceptions

Despite the propaganda from Soviet ideologists that religion in the modern Soviet Union plays a subordinate role, in fact, the Soviet Union is experiencing a religious renaissance.

One way to appreciate the religious sentiments of the Soviet people is to organize the different people groups into seven religious orientations: Christian, Muslim, Buddhist, Jew, Shamanist, Atheist, and modern western sects.

a. Christianity

Among Christians, most believers are orthodox. The two orthodox churches, Russian Orthodox and Georgian Orthodox, include Russians, Ukrainians, Belorussians, Veps, Karelians, Komi, Udmurts, Mari, Mordvins, Chuvashs, Yakuts, and others.

Other people groups of the Northern Region also have large groups of orthodox believers. Most of these groups were Christianized in the 19th century. Smaller groups of Estonians and Latvians have also been integrated into the Russian Orthodox Church.

In the 1,000 years of its existence, the Russian Orthodox Church has experienced several divisions. The largest was during the reign of Peter the Great when the church split into two major sects: the Staroobriadzi (Old-Believers) and the Modernizers. To this day there are still a large number of Staroobriadzi. One can find churches of the Staroobriadzi among the Russians, Ukrainians, Belorussians, and also among some people groups of Siberia.

During the period of the Revolution, a new division occurred in the official Orthodox church. The resulting Renewal Church was not only oppressed by the State but also by the official traditional Church.

Some people groups that belong to the Orthodox Church, over the course of time, have developed their own unique traditions such as the Bulgarians, Rumanians, Moldavians and Greeks.

Out of the different Orthodox groups many sects developed. Some of these sects increased to over a million followers, as did the Dukhoborz, Molokans and the Khlesty.

The Roman Catholic Church has followers from among the eastern Slavs, like the Ukrainians and the Belorussians, and from among the western Slavs, like the Poles and the Czechs. The Lithuanians, Latvians, and Germans are also numbered among the Roman Catholics.

The Lutheran and the Reformed Church include the Estonians, Latvians, Finns, Hungarians, and the Germans.

The Mennonites are primarily Germans while the Methodists are found only in Estonia.

The Evangelical Christians-Baptists consist of numerous people groups and conduct worship services in 22 languages representing 40 different ethnic groups in the Soviet Union.

The Pentecostal churches have reached the most "traditional" Christian people groups in the Soviet Union. They are known for having started mission work in Asia among the Islamic population.

The Adventists are active among the Russians, Ukrainians and other European nations.

The Protestant denominations that work in the Soviet Union, which number over 100, have only a small membership.

b. Islam

Islam is the second largest religious group in the country. Thirty-three people groups profess one or another sect of Islam. Almost all sects of modern Islam are represented in the Soviet Union. There is very little information available about some Islamic groups, such as the Sufi-Brotherhood.

The Sunnite Muslims are primarily represented among the Turkish people groups and those people groups residing in the Caucasus.

The Shiite Muslims have less adherents in the Soviet Union. Shiites may be found among the Azerbaidzhans, Talyshs, Kurds, and Islamic Tatars.

The Ismailite Muslims may be found among most Pamir people, while among the Caucasus Kurds, the Jesids are found.

c. Judaism

The Jewish religion includes many ethnic Jews as well as the Bukharan (Central Asian Jews), the Karaims, and a small number of Tatars.

d. Buddhists-Lamaists

Lamaistic Buddhism originally comes from Tibet. The Tibetan monks brought their religion to the Buryats, Kalmuks, Tuvins, and Khalkha-Mongolians. In addition, some of the Soviet Chinese and Koreans are also Buddhists.

e. Shamanism

There are only a few Shamanistic groups among the people groups in Siberia in the high north and in the northern part of the Ural Mountains. For the inhabitants of the Taiga and Tundra, life has always been a battle for survival. They connect spirits to natural phenomena and believe that survival depends upon a balance between the natural and the supernatural. The difficult assignment of obtaining a balance was given to the Shamans, animistic priests and medicine men.

In South Siberia, Shamanism became mixed with some Buddhist elements. Shamanistic convictions have also survived under a Christian guise among people groups which were Christianized by the Russian Orthodox Church. This process of integration of the natural religions was encouraged and supported by the Orthodox missionaries.

Young people, especially, disappointed by the empty promises of scientific atheism, look back to natural religions.

f. Atheism

The Soviet propaganda apparatus boasts that the majority of the Soviet population is atheistic. To what extent this statement is confirmed by reality is difficult to say. The number of atheistic-minded youth is probably very high. They grew up under the teaching of Marx and Lenin and are rarely exposed to alternative perspectives.

Soviet atheism has all the characteristics of a religion. It has an irrational concept of salvation with rituals and rules of faith, even gods and saints.

Today, a strong wave of disappointment is spreading across the country. Many promises were not fulfilled and the hoped for new society of human brotherhood is far from becoming a reality.

g. Modern Western Sects

The influence of modern western sects, such as the Hare Krishna, is increasing more and more in the Soviet Union. Jehovah's Witnesses are also experiencing growth and popularity.

2. The Situation of Churches in the Soviet Union

2.1 Overview

According to statistics available in the West, the number of Christians in different Christian churches is close to one-third of the total population of the Soviet Union. Of this one-third, approximately 22% are practicing Christians.

The Christians of the Orthodox Church represent about 16.4% of the population. The 45.6 million Orthodox believers belong to 43 different denominations, the largest of which are the Russian Orthodox Church (37 million), the Georgian Orthodox Church (2.5 million), and the Armenian Catholic Church (3 million).

The Christians of the Roman Catholic Church represent about 3.2% of the total population, or about 9 million. However, this number is hard to verify because many Slavic Catholics are counted as Russian Orthodox.

Protestant Christians represent 2.6% of the population, or 7.3 million. Like the Roman Catholic population, this number is also hard to verify because many Protestant groups are not registered. The largest groups are the Evangelical Christians-Baptists (800,000), Pentecostals (300,000), Lutherans (400,000), Reformed (100,000) and Adventists (50,000).

The total number of the evangelicals in the Soviet Union is about 2.5%. This does not include evangelical Orthodox and Catholic believers.

2.2 The Church in the Context of Socialism

The church in the Soviet Union must be understood in the context of socialism; it is a church in an atheistic world hostile to religion. The 70 years of Soviet dictatorship have been cruel and tyrannous years for the beleaguered church. The number of martyrs are in the millions and include lay people, priests, and pastors. It is possible that no other contemporary church has suffered more than the church in the Soviet Union.

The separation of church and state, which began in 1918, gave Christian churches only temporary freedom. However, Stalin's laws governing religious life, enacted in 1929, prohibited almost all organized church activities. Religious education of children and charity ministries became prohibited for the church. Of course, active mission and evangelization were not allowed.

The attacks of the atheistic rulers did not destroy the Church of Jesus Christ. It not only survived but also reveals, in almost all of the denominations, spiritual growth like never before. Although the number of church members has declined, it is primarily because nominal Christians have stopped attending churches. The number of evangelicals, on the other hand, has grown. One hundred years ago there were no evangelicals in Russia; today, the Evangelical Christians-Baptists alone have worship services in 22 languages. The true church of Jesus Christ is strengthened through persecution.

2.3 Registered and the Non-Registered

The religious landscape has changed significantly since 1960. Since the 1960s, initiative groups from different denominations have disregarded the Soviet laws regulating religion and have organized an underground church.

The Evangelical Christians-Baptists initiative group is the best known underground church in the West. At a high point, this group had more than 100,000 members spread among 3,000 churches. Today, these churches belong to the Church Council of the Evangelical Christians-Baptists (CCECB).

In other denominations, initiative groups were also established. All these groups became known to us as the non-registered churches and are sometimes simply referred to as underground church.

Members of these groups have experienced terrible times of persecution. For example, if added together, members of the CCECB have accumulated more than 6,000 years in prisons and labor camps. Other Christians have not had it much better.

On the one hand, it is important to mention that non-registered churches did not exclusively come from the initiative groups. Many churches from different denominations tried over many years to register, but they were not successful. For example, many denominational churches in the Volga area tried to register but were driven by the State to exist illegally and were then persecuted.

On the other hand, many registered churches have also suffered; often not less than the non-registered churches. According to the law, for example, all educational work was prohibited and where it happened it was illegal. Today, in the time of Gorbachev's perestroika, or the "new democratization," many non-registered churches are applying for registration. Among them are some initiative churches which usually register as independent, autonomous churches. This creates some tensions among denominational leaders. This explains why there will probably be new denominations arising in the near future. This is true especially for the Evangelical Christians-Baptists and Pentecostals.

Surprising to some people, the "old-registered" churches are becoming active. Their leadership tends to be flexible and the local churches are developing more and more evangelistic activities. The belief, often propagated in the West, that registered is to non-registered as spiritual is to not spiritual, no longer holds. Spiritual life has developed in both groups and the denominational structures seem unable to resist it.

2.4 General Problems in the Christian Churches

Today, all denominations in the Soviet Union are confronted with a number of problems. Seven of the most prominent are as follows.

a. Problem of Unity

The 70 years of the Soviet rule has left deep marks of distrust among

Christians. Distrust has almost become a distinguishing feature of the Soviet Christians. This is true of all denominations; whether the churches grew, showed life, or were persecuted, they showed more and more distrust of each other. In this area, the atheists celebrate one of their greatest achievements.

The enormous challenge facing missions in the Soviet Union will require unity among Christians. Christians in the Soviet Union have already realized this need. The Evangelical Christians-Baptists, for example, have conducted "Days of Unity" in recent years where they prayed for unity and reconciliation.

b. Insufficient Biblical Theological Training of Leaders

From the very beginning, Soviet leaders have tried to present Christians as dumb and uneducated. In order to make their argument more believable, they reduced pastoral training to a minimum. The following statistics speak for themselves.

The Russian Orthodox Church, with a membership of over 37 million, has only three seminaries and two academies with 2,500 students. The Georgian Orthodox, Armenian Catholic, Lithuanian Catholic, and Estonian Lutheran Churches each have only one institution of higher learning. In all of these seminaries, the historical-critical methods, which engender a great deal of skepticism, are applied to the Biblical texts.

The 600,000 Evangelical Christian-Baptists have no theological school, although there are some prospects for a future seminary. Their pastors receive an insufficient education on an extension basis. Other Churches, such as the Pentecostals, Mennonites, Methodists, and Reformed, have absolutely no theological training available to them.

c. Need for Basic Christian Literature

Much has been written about the need for Bibles in the Soviet Union. What is officially printed in the Soviet Union is not sufficient to meet the demand; nor is the literature which comes from the West.

Especially catastrophic is the situation in the Orthodox and the Catholic Churches which do not have a sufficient supply network in the West. In the past, Christians who ask for a Bible have had to wait for years or pay very high prices on the black market. Even worse, the traditionally non-Christian people groups have almost no portion of the Bible available.

The need for Bibles is paralleled by the need for songbooks, liturgical literature, and especially Biblical and theological literature. The Samizdat-Productions (secret self-printing by the underground church) cannot produce enough evangelistic or theological literature by itself.

d. Need for Space

The church has lost more than 90% of its facilities through Stalin's, Khruchev's, and Brezhnev's actions. Many churches were closed and transformed into storage houses, theaters, cultural centers, or even swimming pools. Sometimes they were simply destroyed.

Today, all denominations find themselves with an enormous need for more space. The 2,500,000 Georgians have only 40 churches left. The Evangelical Christians-Baptists, which number a couple of million people in Moscow and Leningrad, received permission for only one church facility. The church cannot continue in this way. In the process of Gorbachev's "democratization," many church facilities have been given back to the churches. Hopefully, this process will continue.

e. Prohibition on Christian Education for Children

The religious law of 1929 explicitly prohibits Christian education for children by the church or its representatives, even when those representatives are the parents themselves. The educational function of the church was removed by a simple legislative act. Children and youth ministries are only possible on the edge of legality. This situation has been painful for all churches, but especially for those churches where religious education is understood as a necessary part of being and becoming a Christian. Hopefully, this prohibition will change with new laws on religious activities.

f. Restrictions on Evangelistic Activities

The Soviet constitutional law guarantees freedom of speech to all citizens, yet it prohibits all religious information. The churches have been condemned to silence. In contrast, atheists have used all available media in the country. In fact, the promotion of an atheistic world-view is part of the normal curriculum at all levels of education.

In the past, the church has not had legal opportunity to publicly present its views and teaching. With a revision of the law on religious affairs, which is now anticipated, this situation may change.

g. Restrictions on Diaconal Activities

The very nature of the church includes acts of kindness. And yet, the Soviet leaders have not allowed Christians to organize any charitable activities. Thus, the church has had severely limited social involvement. But, where organized social work was impossible, personal testimonies by Christians has played an important role. It is known that Christian acts of kindness and love have often played a role in the conversion of unbelievers.

2.5 Problems of Single Denominations

Single denominations face a number of specific problems in addition to the general problem in the churches. During the first years after the October Revolution, the Russian Orthodox Church experienced the most painful division in its existence. The Soviets supported, and still support, the conservative wing of the Orthodox Church. Other groups have been strongly persecuted. But the different churches of the so-called "Renewal Church" have survived until today. The official church did not integrate them.

The Renewal Church has established their own publications, youth and adult seminars, house groups, and discussion circles. Within these alternative structures, there is a search for the Biblical roots of the true church. This process of new orientation has just started and we eagerly await some of its results.

The national churches of the Gruzians (Georgians) and Armenians have developed into centers of nationalism. That is, nationalists have joined the churches in order to preserve their sense of ethnic and cultural identity threatened by the Soviet occupation. Unfortunately, this means that the churches become the bears of culture and spiritual life tends to be sacrificed.

It is different with the Roman Catholic Church and with the Protestant-Lutheran Church in Latvia and Estonia. Although issues of nationalism also exists in these churches, they experience Christian renewal and awakening. The Oasis Movement (one such renewal movement) has deeply influenced Polish Catholics. People have started to ask about the value of the Bible and about a personal relationship with God.

The Evangelical Christians-Baptists seem to continue to suffer from the separation of their churches into registered and non-registered that happened more than 25 years ago. Autonomous registration of some Initiative-Churches have not been able to bridge the gap created by the division. Nevertheless, the churches are growing despite the problems. Today, they preach the Word of God in 22 different languages. They have started to discover mission and evangelism. This is particularly true of the younger generation of believers who are tired of the never ending registration debates. Some churches are making their first mission plans to enter into Islamic areas. Unfortunately, they do not have the needed means and Biblical theological training.

The Pentecostal churches are also active in missions. They are the fastest growing denomination in the Soviet Union today. The best example of their efforts may be seen in the Caucasus (Armenia), Ukraine, and Baltic States. In recent years, many gypsies have become Christians. The biggest problem for the Pentecostals has been their insufficient teaching and their inability to unify. Accurate data about the different Pentecostal groups is not available. However, it is believed that Biblical, theological education for the pastors and church leaders would help stabilize and unite them.

Today, many German Mennonites, Evangelical Christians-Baptists, and the Lutherans are emigrating. This wave of emigration has created some serious problems within the churches. This is especially true of the multinational churches where the Germans are in leadership. Often such churches are left without pastoral leadership.

3. The Missionary Challenge

3.1 The Challenge for Churches in the East and West

The Christian church in the Soviet Union faces a huge missionary challenge. This can be seen on the mission map of the world. There are large white spots which represent the unreached people groups in this country. Additionally, one must add to these spots the unreached social groups within the population. In facing this challenge, churches need to re-evaluate their role in missions. This evaluation is two-fold.

First, Christians outside of the Soviet Union need to understand that the church in a communist environment is not a defenseless victim, but an outpost of God's Kingdom. The church is called to be God's messenger in the midst of suffering and persecution; it is a powerful tool in the hands of God.

In the West, we have thought almost exclusively about prisoners and persecution. But should not the Church of Jesus Christ think more intensively about God's power and His Great Commission to the Church? It is not right to only have compassion for the church in the Soviet Union. God designed a special purpose for the Soviet Christians and that is not easy to fulfill. Nevertheless, God wants to show His power through the Soviet Christians so that all nations might come to realize that He is Lord. Churches in communist countries do not need us to feel sorry for them; they need our support to fulfill the Great Commission of Jesus Christ.

There has been a dramatic shift in our priorities over the last decades. Instead of thinking about missions, we have thought too much about how bad the Communists have been. The tremendous mission need for the Soviet Union ought to challenge us to re-define our priorities. The Word of God must have the most significant role in this challenge; not our politics, feelings, or even pity.

Second, the church in the Soviet Union must also discover this new mission priority. During the years of persecution, the Soviet Christians have invested a great deal in survival; mission became a matter of minor importance. How did it happen that large evangelical church existed in Islamic areas without attempting to evangelize the Islamic population?

The church in the Soviet Union has to learn to cross its national and social boundaries and begin to practice cross-cultural evangelism. There are still over 100 people groups in the Soviet Union waiting for the first messengers of the Gospel. Christians must develop a heart for the needs of the atheists, Muslims, Buddhists, and nominal Christians. Their intercessory prayers need include the missionary dimension. By this means, God will show them ways and opportunities for successful missionary activities.

3.2 The Un-Reached People Groups in the Soviet Union.

More than 130 people groups live in the Soviet Union. Approximately 70 of these groups have a written language. Only a small portion of these groups come from a Christian background. Although the "Christian" people groups represent the majority of the population, many of the smaller groups have never heard the Gospel. No one has tried to seriously evangelize them; they have been forgotten by the churches in both the East and the West.

The forgotten millions in the Soviet Union can be divided in three major groups: the Muslims, the Siberian people, and the Buddhists.

The Muslims represent the majority. There are 50,000,000 Muslims in 33 different people groups. The Islamic population generally grows much faster than the other people groups. Most of these groups were never evangelized in the past. It is sad that Bible translations are available for only a few groups among the Muslims.

The Siberian people groups are smaller in comparison to the Muslims. The majority of the 25 groups were Christianized in the past by the Russian Orthodox Church. Unfortunately, the people continued to live according to their old ways of life. Today, very little fruit is evident from the work of the Russian Orthodox Church among these groups. There have been attempts by some evangelical churches in the 1920s to evangelize tribes. Today, no mission work is carried on in Siberia.

The four Buddhistic groups — Buriats, Kalmiks, Tuvins, and Chalcha-Mongolians — have probably never heard the gospel; although there are reports that mission work had been done by the Orthodox Church among Buriats.

In additions to these three groups, there are also other people groups which have never heard the gospel, such as the Jews.

3.3 The Un-Reached Social Groups

Not only are different people groups out of reach for the evangelical mission, but also some social groups. The Soviet socialization process has tended to push the church to the margins of society. Evangelicals have developed their own subculture. These factors make it nearly impossible for some social groups to contact the church. The unreached social groups include: academically trained people, artists, actors, musicians, and other representatives of the upper class.

3.4 Reflections on a Mission Strategy

Mission in the Soviet Union must be done exclusively by the churches in the Soviet Union. But the church is not equipped or trained for this task and it needs help from the churches in the West. This help must be motivational and practical.

Strategically, the following areas of help could be significant:

a. Analyzing the situation in the Soviet Union and then presenting the need for mission by means of radio and personal contacts.

b. Translating and distributing both portions of the Bible and the entire Bible into languages of the various people groups.

c. Producing and transporting good evangelical literature in different languages.

d. Producing literature for different social groups.

e. Producing and transporting Christian video films and slide presentations in different languages of the people.

f. Starting Biblical-theological education for church leaders and mission minded people.

g. Conducting information seminars about the culture, religion, and ways for effective mission in the country.

h. Developing a prayer group network for specific regions in the Soviet Union.

By active support from churches in the West, believers in the Soviet Union could be encouraged to face the mission challenge. There are no prohibitions for Christians to move to different parts of the country and to start a tent-making ministry as did the apostle Paul (Acts 18:3). The Soviet state even looks for volunteers in many areas of the unreached peoples, like the Siberian Taiga, Altai, and Pamir Mountains. It is crucial that the churches realize the importance of such mission work and support it. The work of native missionaries must also be supported with prayer from the free world.

Additionally, one could start direct mission work in the Soviet Union from outside. Radio ministry in different languages could be one means of involvement in the country by Christians from outside. Other forms of involvement may come from Christian students (especially from the Third World countries), business people, workers, engineers from Western companies, embassy employees, scientists, and tourists. The involvement of foreigners in the Soviet Union is good, but we must remember that intelligent involvement requires training, especially about the country, people, and church of the Soviet Union.

PART II

PRAYER FOR THE PEOPLE

IN THE SOVIET UNION

1. The Slavic People

The largest nations in the Soviet Union belong to the Slavic language family. Three East Slavic groups — the Russians, Ukrainians, and Belorussians — represent three-fourths of the total Soviet population. In their traditional settlements, they represent 95% of the population.

Smaller, mostly West Slavic nationalities, such as the Poles, Czechs, Slovaks, and Bulgarians, play only a modest role. Culturally, they belong to other Slavic states and over the centuries have opposed Russian demands.

The differences between the East and the West Slavic people is observed not only in population, but also in religious perspectives. The East Slavs belong to the Orthodox Church; the West Slavs are predominantly Roman Catholic, although some are Protestant.

Politically, the West Slavs have been pushed into a societal insignificance. As a result, the process of russification is increasing and produces some anti-Russian, nationalistic movements.

Russians are the lords in the land. All central positions in politics, business, military, and the party are occupied by Russians. Their culture and language have the leading position in the Soviet society, even if it means subjugating other highly developed cultures, such as the Baltic peoples's culture.

Russian is the trade language and is spoken by more than 50% of the non-Russian population. The Ukrainians and the Belorussians also have a significant role in the Soviet society because of their large populations.

Among the Slavs, the Russian Orthodox Church, with its 37 million members, does not present a unified picture. Most of the members are nominal Christians. However, all of the East Slavic people have experienced revival in the past centuries. The evangelical churches have about 2 million followers. More than half of those believers are Ukrainians. And, as explained above, the majority of the evangelical Christians belong to the lower social class of the Soviet society.

There are also some evangelical Christians among the Poles, Czechs, Slovaks, and Bulgarians. Predominately, they belong to Russian or Ukrainian churches.

Mission Concerns:

There are some large Slavic evangelical churches. These churches are growing and, particularly in the Ukraine, mission activity is increasing. But, they are only able to reach into the middle class in a limited way. They do not reach the higher social class of the population. The churches have established their own culture and have a hard time differentiating between their own culture and the Gospel. This has had a negative influence on mission.

Because the churches have a strong "Slavic" influence and orientation, the non-Slavic members tend to be pushed into becoming "Slavic" themselves. As a result, missions has had a negative influence among the non-Slavic groups. It is sad that only a few Slavs have been motivated to do missions among their own Slavic people and country. These forgotten nations of the Soviet Union are not yet on a church agenda.

The process of russification of the evangelical Slavs has had a negative influence on evangelistic efforts among the West Slavs. There is a need to plant ethnic churches that use their own languages.

In general, the Slavic Christians who are motivated to missionize are lacking the necessary means and knowledge for effective evangelism. In this area, churches in the free world could provide some assistance.

Ethnic Overview of Chapter 1-4

Nordpolarmeer

H.I. Taimyr

Jamal H.I.

H.I. Kamtschatka

Sachalin

Aral See

Kaspisches Meer

Schwarzes Meer

1.1 = Russians   2 = Lithuanians
1.2 = Ukrainians   3 = Moldavians and Rumanians
1.3 = Belorussians   4 = Caucasians

1.1 The Russians

Population: 137,397,000
Language group: Slavic languages
Language: Russian
Region: Central European part of the Soviet Union, additionally in almost all parts of the country
Capital: Moscow
Religion: 30% Russian Orthodox; Christian Sects about 1%
Evangelicals: about 1.5%
Bible translation: available

Information:

The Russians are the largest people group in the Soviet Union. They are found in almost all regions and their language is the official trade language. The Russians have been Christians for 1000 years, but the official Orthodox Church has become only a traditional church without a genuine relationship to the people. The Russian Bible was translated approximately 110 years ago. Revivals followed. Presently, the evangelical groups number about two million followers. Despite the atheistic propaganda during the past 70 years, today the Russians are more open to the Gospel, especially in the cities. Russians are found throughout the Soviet Union and have an ability to adjust to other cultures. As a result, they are an excellent channel for evangelism in the Soviet Union. Unfortunately, the Russians are sometimes identified with the Soviet regime and despised, especially in the western and southern parts of the Soviet Union.

Prayer Concern:

1 Awakening interest in missions in the Russian evangelical churches for the unreached levels in the nation: the intellectuals, the youth and the secularized Orthodox people.
2. Theological education for the evangelical churches.
3. Bible distribution for the religious searching.
4. Evangelism work among students.
5 Church planting in Urban centers.

1.2 The Ukrainians

Population: 42,347,000
Language group: Slavic language
Language: Ukrainian
Region: Ukrainian SSR in the western part of the Soviet Union; additionally, they are found in almost all other areas in the USSR. There are also 1.7 million Ukrainians outside of the USSR
Capital: Kiev
Religion: Russian Orthodox; Catholic; Protestant
Evangelicals: about 1 million
Bible translation: available

Information:

Despite a century long association with Russians, the Ukrainians have maintained their national identity. The West Ukrainians are especially known for their national pride. The Ukrainians, together with the Russians, are the leading nationalities in the Soviet Union.

The Ukrainians are considered Christians. In the East Ukraine, there tend to be more Russian Orthodox; in the West, there tend to be more Catholics and members of the United Church. They are less secularized than the Russians and more open to the Gospel. There are many evangelically oriented churches in the Ukraine. The fastest growth is seen among the Evangelical Christians-Baptists and Pentecostals. Other sects, such as the Jehovah's Witnesses, are also rapidly growing.

Prayer Concerns:

1. Revival in the Orthodox and the Catholic churches.
2. Strengthening the mission work in the evangelical churches among the Ukrainians.
3. Radio Broadcasting from TWR in the Ukrainian language.
4. Theological education for pastors and church leaders in Ukrainian language.
5. Production, transportation, and distribution of different Christian literature, especially in big cities.
6. Conversion of Ukrainian intellectuals.

Russian

Ukrainian

Belorussian

1.3 The Belorussians

Population: 9,463,000
Language group: Slavic languages
Language: Belorussian
Region: Belorussian SSR in the Western part of the Soviet Union;
additionally, they are also in the Baltic, Siberia, and Kazakistan.
Capital: Minsk
Religion: Christianity; Russian Orthodox; Roman Catholic; Protestant.
Evangelicals: about 120,000
Bible translation: available

Information:

The Belorussians belong to the East Slavic group of the Slavic language group. For centuries they were active in agriculture and cattle breeding. There are more people working in Belorussia in agriculture than in any other Soviet republic. Forests and moors make work difficult, and the standard of living is lower, for example, than in the Ukraine.

This explains the massive exodus from this land. Today, over one million people live in cities and many have left their own country in a search for better living conditions.

The Belorussians are traditionally Orthodox or Catholics. In the country, superstition is widespread. But, secularism has also entered the homes with the process of urbanization. Around the turn of the century, the Belorussians experienced some revival periods. Today one finds growing churches.

Prayer Concerns:

1. Strengthening of the Evangelical churches and awakening of a mission awareness for their own people.
2. Starting missions work with house churches in the cities.
3. Starting mission work aimed at students.
4. Starting a radio broadcast in Belorussian.
5. Establishing a Biblical, theological training program for pastors and church leaders.

1.4 The Poles

Population: 1,151,000
Language group: Slavic language
Language: Polish
Region: western parts of the Ukraine, Belorussia, and Lithuanian Republic
Religion: Roman Catholics 80%; Orthodox 15%
Evangelicals: 5%
Bible translation: available

Information:

The Polish people in the Soviet Union represent a Slavic minority and one does not talk about their bitter past. They live in an area that belonged to Poland prior to 1939 when it became occupied. This chapter of history is still closed. Accordingly, this is reflected in the relationship between Poles and the Soviet state. Pushed into a political abstinence, Poles often find their refuge in religion. The Polish Catholics in the Soviet Union are alive and well. The evangelical churches, such as the Evangelical Christians-Baptists and the Pentecostals, also show some remarkable signs of life. The relationship between Poland and the Poles of the Soviet Union has definitely influenced the life of the Polish church in the U.S.S.R.

Prayer Concerns:

1. Building up Biblical based churches among converted Catholics.
2. Biblical, theological education for pastors and church leaders.
3. Developing and expanding contacts to their homeland, Poland.
4. Opening up the Polish church for missions among the unreached peoples in the Soviet Union.
5. Expanding from video-evangelism to relational evangelism teams.

1.5 The Czechs and the Slovaks

Population: Slovaks (9,400); Czechs (18,000)
Language Group: Slavic language
Language: Slovak and Czech
Region: Transkarpatia (Karpato-Ukraine)
Religion: Christianity/Roman Catholics
Evangelicals: unknown
Bible translation: available

Information:

The Transkarpatian area is predominantly settled by the Czechs and the Slovaks. This area was occupied by the Soviet Union in 1945. In order to justify this occupation, the government has systematically introduced its policies of russification. The national minorities have been pushed to the margin of societal existence. For many of them, the church became a symbol of national identity. It is sad to say that the local evangelical churches in the Zakarpatiie (Transkarpatian) area have not yet recognized their need to reach the people of their own language and culture with the gospel. The believing Czechs and Slovaks are thereby pushed into becoming members in Russian or Ukrainian churches. And, unfortunately, membership in such churches means that the believing Czechs and Slovaks tend to be alienated by their own people.

Prayer Concern:

1. Print and transport Bibles in Czech and Slovak languages.
2. Start radio broadcasts in Czech and Slovak languages for these minority groups in the Soviet Union.
3. Awaken the Czech and Slovak believers to a mission to their own people.
4. Establish Czech and Slovak house groups and churches in their own language.

1.6 The West Ukrainians

Population: unknown
Language Group: Slavic language
Language: Ukrainian
Region: western part of the Ukrainian SSR
Evangelicals: 5%
Bible translation: available

Information:

The West Ukrainians include the Lemky, Boiki, Gutsul, Litvins, and Polishchuk. Part of the Western Ukraine was added to the U.S.S.R. in 1939-1940 and the remainder in 1945. The people groups of this area strongly opposed the Soviet and Ukrainian influence. As a result, they maintain a strong cultural and ethnic independence.

The majority of West-Ukrainians are peasants. They tended to remain on the land rather than urbanize; this helps explain the conservative spirit among West Ukrainians. Despite this strong conservative position, many have left the traditional Orthodox or Roman Catholic Churches, and have become members in living churches. The Pentecostals have had a huge influence on those living in the West Ukraine.

Prayer Concerns:

1. Stabilization of the evangelical churches in the West Ukraine.
2. Biblical theological education for the church leadership.
3. Revival in the traditional churches.
4. Planting new churches in areas without evangelical churches.

1.7 The Bulgarians

Population: 365,000
Language Group: Slavic language
Language: Bulgarians
Region: southwestern Ukraine and southern Moldavia
Evangelical: several thousand
Bible translation: available

Information:

Bulgarians have an ancient cultural heritage. The first Bulgarian state was formed in 681 A.D. Beginning in the 14th century, the Turks occupied this region until the beginning of the 20th century. This era deeply influenced the language and culture of the Bulgarians.

Today, the Soviet Bulgarians live in areas which originally did not belong to the Soviet Union. Their existence is preferably not mentioned by the Soviets and they experience difficulties in these regions. For this reason, many Bulgarians have left this region for other parts of the Soviet Union.

Although there are several thousand Bulgarian Christians in the Soviet Union, there does not exist a Bulgarian Evangelical church.

Prayer Concerns:

1. Awaken interest in mission and evangelism by Bulgarian believers for their own people.
2. Transport Bulgarian Bibles and evangelistic literature to the USSR.
3. Plant Bulgarian-speaking churches in areas with a large Bulgarian population.

2. The Baltic People

The two Baltic Republics of Lithuania and Latvia were added to the Soviet Union in 1940. This forceful integration cost many people their freedom and sometimes their lives. Almost one million Baltic people were forced to leave their homeland and were transported to Siberia. This is not forgotten in the Baltic.

In both republics, people find national support in their churches. The Lithuanian Roman Catholic Church registers one of the highest church attendances in the Soviet Union. Many priests see themselves as representing the cause of the common people. This is one reason why the State sharply criticizes the church. The Roman Catholic Church, in addition to the Evangelical Christians-Baptists, has had the most number of persecuted Christians. The relationship between the State and the Lutheran Church of Latvia is also tense and, recently, even more tensions have arisen. The state has responded by extraditing priests.

The Baltic Churches are not only places for political and national debates, many churches have also experienced spiritual renewal. Young people are again asking for God and His Word. The independent, evangelical churches are strengthened most from this renewal. But, reports of this renewal are mixed. At the time when the Baptists in Latvia are still busy with solving some traditional questions, the Pentecostals are spreading rapidly. The Pentecostal churches in Lithuania are also known for their work among drug addicted people and, in other areas, Baptists have started evangelistic groups. Most of them are charismatic and tend not to be supported by church leadership.

There are almost no independent, evangelical churches in Lithuania, however. Although the oldest Baptist Church is located in Memel-Klaipeda, the evangelicals were not able to influence the predominantly Catholic population. But, in the last couple of years, new small churches have been planted.

Mission Challenge:

The people groups in the Baltic need a new Reformation. In many places people pray for revival. The traditional churches, and also the evangelical churches, need to find new ways to reach the atheism-disappointed and occupied population.

Additionally, the Christians in the Baltics have lost the heart to missionize the different groups in the Soviet Union. They tend not to be concerned about other groups which come to their republics through the resettlement policies. In fact, there is some animosity toward foreign people.

Nevertheless, the foreigners in Latvia and Lithuania must hear the Gospel. And, through their connections with Western Europe, the Latvians and Lithuanians could be a good channel for mission to the unreached people groups in the Soviet Union.

2.1 The Lithuanians

Population: 2,851,000
Language group: Baltic Language
Language: Lithuanian
Region: Lithuanian SSR and the boarder areas. Approximately 320,000 live in the West, especially the United States.
Capital: Vilnius
Religion: 90% Christian/Catholics; 10% atheists
Evangelicals: 0.5%
Bible translation: available

Information:

The Lithuanians call themselves Lietuviai. They are Catholics.

Lithuania was forcefully added to the Soviet Union in 1940. Since then it has been a republic full of political unrest. The Rebublic's strong opposition to the Soviet ideology has been attributed to its relationship with the Catholic Church. However, Lithuanian Catholicism is strongly mixed with superstition and non-evangelical beliefs. The worship of Mary plays an important role. In many areas, Catholicism is mixed with occult practices. For this reason, evangelicals have had almost no success in Lithuania. In recent times, there has been a religious awakening among the Lithuanians, particularly among the young people who seem to be open to the Gospel.

Prayer Concerns:

1. Conversion of Catholic priests and church planting.
2. Opening the existing evangelical churches for evangelism among their own people.
3. Strengthening the existing evangelism teams.
4. Starting work among the Lithuanian students.
5. Developing, printing, and transporting good literature for evangelistic purposes in the Lithuanian language.

Lithuanian

Latvian

2.2 The Latvians

Population: 1,439,000
Language group: Baltic languages
Language: Latvian
Region: Latvian SSR, but also in other Baltic Republics.
Capital: Riga
Religion: Christianity; Lutherans, Catholics, and independent churches
Evangelicals: about 100,000
Bible translation: available

Information:

Latvia has belonged to the Soviet empire since 1940. Many Latvians lost their lives during the time of the forced occupation. Thousands of Latvians were deported to Siberia. The systematic russification continues to this day. For this reason, the nationally conscious Latvians have only a limited chance to advance in their careers.

Many Latvians are politically disappointed and turn to religion and the church. A spiritual awakening is not only seen among the Baptists and Pentecostals, but also in the Lutheran and Catholic Churches. These trends open an exciting opportunity for the Gospel.

Prayer Concern:

1. For a break through revival in Latvia.
2. Protection for evangelistically active pastors and priests.
3. Networking among active Christians.
4. Development, transportation, and distribution of good Christian literature in the Latvian language.
5. Theological education for pastors and church leaders.
6. Christian broadcasts in the Latvian language.

3. The Rumanian People

The Rumanian people are represented in the Soviet Union by two groups: the Rumanians and the Moldavians. The Moldavians are considered to be a subgroup of the Rumanian people. Only after the occupation of the Bessarabia, in 1940, did they become an independent people group.

For many centuries, the Rumanians have belonged to the Orthodox Church, exhibiting their own unique religious characteristics. Many have come to a personal relationship with God in the past centuries. Today, there are big churches of Evangelical Christians-Baptists and Pentecostals in Moldavia. Different renewal groups from Rumania have also had a strong influence on the development of these churches.

Mission Concerns:

The Moldavian churches are very active among their own people, but they sometimes ignore other people groups which live in this area. Unreached peoples in this area include the Gagauzs, Turks, Bulgarians, and others. In recent years, the first gypsies were converted. This development shows a turning point and we need to include them in our prayers.

In order to do effective mission work among different people groups, the Moldavian Christians will need help from outside of the Soviet Union.

Moldavian

3.1 The Moldavians and the Rumanians

Population: 2,968,000
Language group: Rumanian languages
Language: Moldavian/Rumanian
Region: Moldavian SSR and the bordering areas in the Ukraine and Russia.
Capital: Kishenev
Religion: Christianity; 30% Rumanian Orthodox and 0.25% Protestant
Evangelicals: about 50,000
Bible translation: available

Information:

The Moldavians, or Moldavani as they call themselves, speak a Rumanian dialect. The Moldavian nation was constructed by the Soviet government. But, in a relatively short time the Moldavians have developed a national self-identity. Moldavians who live outside of Moldavia are considered Rumanians, although there is not much difference to the Moldavians.

The Moldavians, or Rumanians, are Rumanian Orthodox believers.

The majority of them do not practice their beliefs, however. Most Moldavians are secularized or belong to other Christian denominations or sects. The strongest evangelical churches are the Evangelical Christians-Baptists and the Pentecostals.

Prayer Concerns:

1. Awaken interest in missions in Moldavian/Rumanian Churches.
2. Develop, produce, and distribute evangelical literature in the Moldavian language.
3. Start radio broadcasts in the Moldavian language.
4. Theological education for Moldavian pastors and church leaders.

4. The Caucasians

The Transcaucasus, an area between the Caspian and the Black Sea, on the border between Asia and Europe, is one of most fascinating ethnographical areas in the world. Approximately 40 different people groups live there. Often these groups speak completely different languages. Thirty-three of the groups belong to the Caucasian language group. The Armenians are also listed with these groups, although they belong to an independent Indo-Germanic language group.

The peoples in the Caucasus not only have different languages, they also have different cultures and religions. Although geographically they are close to each other, they have developed their cultures in diverse ways.

Christianity was introduced in the Caucasus in the third century; since that time the Armenians and Georgians have survived many attacks. The Armenian Catholic and the Georgian Orthodox Churches are the keepers of a national Christian tradition. Additionally, there are some new and vital evangelical churches in Armenia and Georgia. The Evangelical Christian-Baptists and the Pentecostals are very active. In the last five years, one of the young Armenian Pentecostal churches registered a tremendous growth of over 2,000 people. The evangelical Armenians and Georgians are active in missions and have tried to reach their own people with the Gospel of Christ.

Most Caucasians, on the other hand, belong to Islam. Century-long fights with the Armenians and the Georgians, and later the Russians, made it almost impossible to reach these people groups with the Gospel. There has been no real mission work done among them and a Bible translation is not available for most of these groups.

Mission Concerns:

Among the evangelical churches in the Caucasus, a religious awakening has begun that is also strongly mission oriented. Young believers are interested in mission not only for their people but also for other people groups. In order to accomplish this task, they need help from the East and the West. The problem is that for many of the people groups being evangelized, a translation of the Bible is not available. Modern media could be very useful for mission purpose.

Christians need special training for this cross-cultural mission and evangelism effort.

4.1 The Georgians (Gruzians)

Population: 3,433,000
Language group: Caucasian languages
Language: Gruzinian (Georgian)
Region: Caucasus
Capital: Tbilissi
Religion: Christianity/Georgian Orthodox
Evangelicals: several thousand
Bible translation: available

Information:

The Georgians are an ancient people group and have a rich cultural past. Strong tradition defines their lifestyle. The Georgian Orthodox Church, which is 1500 years old, has played an important role in the development of the Georgian culture, especially in the development of literature and art. Despite integration into the USSR, the people of Georgia are still strongly influenced by the church. Unfortunately, there are still many nominal Christians. The evangelical churches, on the other hand, show some growth.

Economically, in addition to agriculture, other industries have developed and are becoming more important. As a result, more and more people live in cities.

Prayer Concerns:

1. Awakening in the Georgian Orthodox Church.
2. Pray for the openness of urban populations to receive the gospel.
3. Intensification of missionary by the Georgian churches for their own people.
4. Print, transport, and distribute Bibles in Georgia.
5. Start Radio Broadcast in Georgian.

Georgian
(Gruzian)

Armenian

4.2 The Armenians

Population: 4,151,000 in the Soviet Union; of those, 2,725,000 live in Armenia.
Language group: Indo-Germanic language
Language: Armenian
Region: Caucasus
Capital: Erivan
Religion: Christianity/Armenian Catholic
Evangelicals: several thousand
Bible translation: available

Information:

Armenians are people of an ancient culture. Their cultural tradition has a strong influence on the life of the people, despite the socialistic influence. The Armenian Catholic Church is an important factor in this tradition. The first Christian influence came to Armenia through Syrians in the second century. In 310 A.D., Christianity became the official state religion and, since 506 A.D., the Armenian Catholic Church has been independent. The church is still very important to most Armenians. To be an Armenian means at the same time to be a member of the Armenian Catholic Church to which 75% of all Armenians belong.

By the turn of the century, the Reformed Church was formed under the influence of foreign missionaries. However, the Baptists and the Pentecostals are also active and record a strengthening of their numbers. The Armenians have been a widely dispersed people as a result of persecution, wars, deportation, and other repressions. This Armenian diaspora accounts for the nearly 2 million Armenians who live in 60 different countries in the world. In the USA many, Armenian Churches are evangelical.

Prayer Concerns:

1. Distribution of Bibles among Armenians.
2. Evangelical churches in Armenia that their efforts bear fruit.
3. For the younger generation, which is more open for the Gospel, so that they might be reached with Christ's message.
4. Revival among the nominal Armenian Catholics.
5. Radio broadcast in the Armenian Language by Trans-World Radio.

4.3 The Chechens

Population: 756,000
Language group: Caucasian Language
Language: Chechen
Region: Chechen-Ingush ASSR in North Caucasus
Capital: Grosnii
Religion: Islam/Sunnite
Christians: none
Bible translation: the Gospel of John and Acts

Information:

The Chechens call themselves "Nakhchuo". They are the largest people group in the North Caucasus and are also the original inhabitants of this region.

Chechens are shepherds and farmers; 80% of all Chechens live in the country. They are characterized by a very expressive tradition and strong family ties.

Folk-Islam, to which the Chechens adhere, is mixture of Islam and animism. Many families still live in fear of the evil spirits of their ancestors. In contrast, the secularized Chechens often lose contact with their own people and mix with Russians and people from other nationalities.

Prayer Concerns:

1. Translation of the whole Bible into the Chechen language.
2. Awakening of the local churches which are in the Chechen areas.
3. Conversion of Chechens in cities; for example, in their capital Grosnyi.
4. Send missionaries into new cities, like Malgokek, Gudermes, Nasrani, Argun, and others.

4.4 The Avars

Population: 483,000
Language group: Caucasian Language
Language: Avar
Region: Dagestan ASSR (North Caucasus) and northwest Azerbaidzhan
Cities: Khasawyurt, Baynaksk
Christians: none
Bible translation: the Gospel of John (1979)

Information:

The Avars call themselves Maarulal and are the largest Dagestani people group. In the past, they have lived in the mountains and were known as hunters and cattle breeders.

Today, most Avars live in the areas of Khasawyurt and Baynaksk. They are predominantly agricultural people. With modernization, many young people tend to move into the cities, and with that, secularization has increased and family ties have deteriorated.

Economically, the Avars are in transition. The oil fields in Dagestan have become depleted and unemployment is high. Unemployment has forced many Avars to leave their traditional regions for other areas, such as Siberia. The Avars are open to the Gospel.

Prayer Concern:

1. Translation of the whole Bible into the language of the Avars.
2. Awakening for mission in the evangelical churches in the area of the Caspian Sea.
3. Send missionaries to the fast growing cities, especially to Khasawyurt and Baynaksk.
4. Conversion of Avars in the cities of Dagestan and other areas in the USSR.

4.5 Small Dagestani People Groups from the Avars

Population: several thousand
Language group: Caucasian language
Language: Tribal languages
Region: Dagestan
Religion: Islam
Christians: none
Bible translation: not available

Information:

The Dagestani people groups include: Andi, Botlig, Godoberi, Bagulal, Akhwakh, Chamalals, Karata, Tindi, Bexheta, Khwarshi, Dido, Ginug, Khunzal, and Archi. These groups of people are officially listed as Avars, but the people themselves reject this. Despite some attempts at unification, these groups maintain their ethnic and language independence.

Geographical conditions support the isolation of the people; the mountains are a natural wall between one group and another. Among families where some members have moved into the cities, the traditions are loosing their hold. This process of urbanization is very slow. The Dagestani people primarily work in agriculture and cattle breeding. Christian mission among these people is yet unknown.

Prayer Concerns:

1. Production and transport of Christian video programs. Employing video films is an excellent way to introduce the Christian faith because the majority of these groups do not have a written language.
2. Awakening of mission interest for these small people groups among the Christian churches who are already located in the Dagestani area.
3. Conversion of more open members of these groups in the cities; especially students who study outside of Dagestan.

4.6 The Lezghian (Lezgin)

Population: 383,000
Language group: Caucasian Language
Language: Lezgin
Region: southeastern Dagestan and northern Azerbaidzhan
Religion: Islam
Christians: not known
Bible translation: not available

Information:

The Lezghi, which is the self-designation of the Lezgins, represent one of the oldest people groups in Dagestan. Until the l9th century, the Lezgin lived in free tribal communities. Only in the 20th century have the Lezgins developed a sense of togetherness. The development of a Lezgin written language was a major factor in this unification process.

The Lezgins love their independence and have defended it in the past. They are more open to hear the gospel than other people groups in Dagestan. One also finds small groups of Lezgins outside of Dagestan. The young people, especially, leave and move to the cities. Detachment from their clan often results in breaking away from traditional religious beliefs. These secularized Lezgins are more receptive to the Gospel.

Prayer Concerns:

1. Translation of the New Testament into the Lezgin language.
2. Production and transportation of Christian literature and video films in the Lezgin language.
3. Awakening of a interest in mission in churches in this region for Lezgins.
4. Sending missionaries to the Lezgins.
5. Conversion of secularized Lezgins outside of Dagestan.

4.7 Smaller Dagestani people groups from the Lezgins

Population: several thousand
Language group: Caucasian language
Language: Tribal languages
Region: southeast Dagestan and northern Azerbaidzhan
Religion: Islam
Christians: none
Bible translation: not available

Information

The Lezgin people groups — Artshinzs, Kiirinzs, Akhtyns, and Kubinzs — still maintain their ethnic differences. At the same time they assimilated, so it is appropriate to speak about Lezgin dialects rather than distinct languages. A solid mission strategy could be applicable to all of these groups without major difficulties. They are, like the Lezgins, in the process of secularization. This secularization process correlates with the trend to urbanize, especially among the youth. Mission activities among these people is unknown.

Prayer Concerns:

1. Translation of the New Testament in the Lezgin language.
2. Awakening interest for missions among Christians in this region for all different Lezgin groups.
3. Conversion of secularized clan members.
4. Sending missionaries to the Lezgin tribes.

4.8 The Dargins

Population: 287,000
Language group: Caucasian language
Language: Dargin
Region: Dagestani ASSR
Capital: Makhatshkala
Religion: Islam/Sunnite
Christians: none
Bible translation: not available

Information:

The Dargins are the mountain inhabitants of Dagestan. They are divided into different people groups which are currently trying to form one nation. The Kubachi and Kaitak are listed by some researchers as independent groups. Additional sub-groupings of the Dargins are the Akusha, Khurkili, Tsudakhar, Sirkhin, and Muerin.

Some of Dargins are isolated, living in far removed valleys. Their religion is mixed with occult and superstitious expressions. Christian missions has never reached these people.

Prayer Concerns:

1. Translation of the Bible into the Dargin language and into the language of some of the major Dargin people groups.
2. Production of Christian video in the Dargin language. That could have great success in some of the far removed villages.
3. Awakening interest among the evangelical churches of Dagestan for missions to the Dargins.

4.9 Small Dagestani People groups from the Dargins

Population: several thousand
Language group: Caucasian language
Language: Tribal languages
Region: mountains of Central Dagestan
Religion: Islam/Sunnite
Christians: none
Bible translation: not available

Information:

The Kubachi, Kaitak, Akusha, Khurkili, Tsudakhar, Sirkhin, and Muerin are officially counted as Dargins; they are all culturally and linguistically related to each other. Nevertheless, they maintain their independence and some researchers consider them to be independent people groups.

They inhabit the valleys of the central Dagestan and generally they work in agriculture and cattle breeding. The majority of these people are bound to the land and, as a result, they are more conservative and conscious of tradition.

Generally, these people groups belong to Islam, although its expression among these groups has unique features that often reflect animistic aspects. Fear of demons and other superstitions are found in many of their villages.

Prayer Concerns:

1. Produce Christian video films and transport them into the villages.
2. Awaken an interest in mission among Christians in this region for the small Dargins people groups.
3. Conversion of some of the members from the different tribes in cities.
4. Conversion of students from different tribes in cities.

4.10 The Ingush

Population: 186,000
Language group: Caucasian language
Language: Ingush
Region: Chechen-Ingush ASSR in the northern Caucasus
Capital: Grosni
Religion: Islam/Sunnite
Christians: none
Bible translation: not available

Information:

Similar to the Chechen, the Ingush represent the original inhabitants of the northern Caucasus. The oldest settlements of the Ingush are found in some valleys in Central Caucasus which are difficult to reach. In the 17th century, Ingush resettled in the valleys of the Sunsha, Assa, and Terek Rivers. This resettlement was supported by the Russian government. The Ingush resisted Russian colonial policies and it was only by the end of the last century when Ingush integrated with the Russian Empire. During World War II, many of the Ingush sympathized with the Germans and were deported to North Kazakistan and Siberia.

Ingush are strongly connected to the land; however, today only 64.6% of them live in the country, probably as a result of the deportation policies. During the deportation, many of the Ingush came in contact with believers as well as German influence. Conversions of Ingush are not known.

Prayer Concerns:

1. Translate the New Testament into the Ingush language.
2. Awaken interest in mission among the German evangelical churches for the Ingush people.
3. Send missionaries into Ingush cities.
4. Conversion of influential Ingush in cities like Grosnij, Malgobek, Nasrani, and others.

4.11 The Lak (Lakzs)

Population: 86,000
Language group: Caucasian language
Language: Lak
Region: central and northern Dagestan ASSR
Religion: Islam/Sunnite
Christians: none
Bible translation: not available

Information:

The Lakzs originally lived along the Kazi Kumukh River. The Lakzs older name of Kazi Kumukh derived from the name of this river. Some of the Lakzs settled in the Northern Dagestan Valley in 1944. This opened them to new ideas. The former cattle breeders changed and began working in agriculture. Lakzs are known for their handcrafted work. Their declining numbers are attributed to their mixing with other Dagestani people groups. However, in recent years there has been an awakening of a national consciousness, manifest in some of their writings. Planted missionary activities among the Lakzs are unknown.

Prayer Concerns:

1. Translate the New Testament in the Lak language.
2. Awaken mission interest among Christians for the Lakzs.
3. Send missionaries to Northern Dagestan where most Lakzs live.
4. Conversion of secularized intellectual Lakzs.

4.12 The Tabasarans

Population: 75,000
Language group: Caucasian language
Language: Tabasaran
Region: southeastern part of Dagestan ASSR, North Caucasus
Cities: Belidshi, Khiv, Derbent
Religion: Islam/Sunnite
Christians: unknown
Bible translation: not available

Information:

The Tabasaran belong to about 30 different people groups which reside in Dagestan. Despite century-long battles with the Russian Czars and the Iranians, and despite the Soviet Infiltration, the Tabasarans have maintained their identity. The Tabasarans belong to the few groups which resisted the Russian colonization the longest. Until the 9th century, Christian elements were found in the Tabasaran culture. Today, the Tabasarans are Muslims.

Tabasarans are known for their tapestries and ornate rugs. This small people group sees itself challenged by the large surrounding nations. They are proud and willing to fight. In their mountain world they feel like rulers.

Prayer Concerns:

1. Translate the Bible into the Tabasaran language.
2. Awaken an interest in mission among the evangelical churches for the Tabasaran.
3. Conversion of the Tabasaranian youth who study outside of their homeland.

4.13 The Rutuls

Population: 15,000
Language group: Caucasian Language
Language: Rutulic
Region: southern parts of Dagestan ASSR and northern parts of Azerbaidzhan SSR
City: Rutul
Religion: Islam/Sunnite
Christians: none
Bible translation: not available

Information:

The Rutuls inhabit areas on the upper part of the Samur River. Culturally and linguistically, the Rutuls are close to the Lezgins from whom they maintained independence despite many relational bounds. Most Rutuls are cattle breeders; sheep breeding is especially popular. Rutuls who work in agriculture appear to be more open to potential missionary work. However, missionary work, as far as we know, has never been done among the Rutuls.

Prayer Concern:

1. Translate the Bible into the Rutuls language.
2. Awaken an interest in mission among Christian churches in the Soviet Union for the Rutuls.
3. Start prayer groups for Rutuls.
4. Conversion of the Rutuls youth in the Soviet Universities.

4.14 The Zackur

Population: 14,000
Language group: Caucasian language
Language: Zakhur
Region: southwestern part Dagestan ASSR; northern Azerbaidzhan SSR.
Religion: Islam/Sunnite
Christians: none
Bible translation: not available

Information:

Ethnically and linguistically, the Zakhurs belong to the Lezgin people group. The Lezgin language is the written language for the Zakhurs, although the Azerbaidzhanian Zachurs use Aseri as their written and trade language. Despite this, there is a strong sense of national identity. Most of the Zachur men are sheep breeders. Their huge sheep herds are known far beyond their own region. Only a few Zachurs are farmers and only a very small group has moved to the cities. Mission work among Zachurs is unknown.

Prayer Concerns:

1. Translate the New Testament into the Lezgin language.
2. Awaken an interest in mission among the Caucasian Christians for the Zachurs.
3. Start a prayer group for the Zachurs.
4. Conversion of secularized Zachurs in cities.

4.15 The Aguls

Population: 10,000
Language group: Caucasian language
Language: Agul
Region: southern part of Dagestan ASSR.
Religion: Islam/Sunnite
Christians: none
Bible translation: not available

Information:

The Aguls are ethnically and linguistically related to the Lezgins. Today, one may distinguish four groups of Aguls who have different dialects: the Agulders, the Kurakhders, the Khushanders, and the Khpiukders. Each of these groups lives in their own valley in South Dagestan. The Aguls are almost exclusively cattle breeders. In villages, people also do some hand crafts. Aguls do not have their own written language; therefore, they use the Lezgin written language which is understood by all Aguls. Mission work among the Aguls is unknown.

Prayer Concerns:

1. Translate the New Testament into the Lezgin language.
2. Awaken an interest in mission among Caucasian Christians for the Aguls.
3. Start evangelistic work among Lezgin people groups in Dagestan.
4. Conversion of Aguls who are in cities.

4.16 The Udin (Udi)

Population: 7,000
Language group: Caucasian Language
Language: Udin
Region: northwestern Azerbaidzhan SSR, northeastern Armenia SSR, and southwestern Georgian SSR
Religion: Christianity; Orthodox and Georgian
Evangelicals: unknown
Bible translation: not available

Information:

The Udi, which is also their self-designation, belong to a Christian minority among the Dagestani people groups. Culturally, they maintain close ties to their big Christian neighbors; the Georgians and the Armenians. For written language, the Udi use Georgian, Armenian, or Aseri.

Traditionally, the Udi are an agricultural people. A significant part of the population works in small industries in cities.

Prayer Concerns:

1. Conversion of nominal Christian Udi and conversion of some of the Orthodox clergy they have contact with.
2. Plant new churches among Udi.
3. Awaken missionary interest among the evangelical churches in Tbilissi (Georgia) for the Udi.
4. Distribute evangelistic literature in the area of Udin.

4.17 The Kabardian (Kabardinian)

Population: 322,000
Language group: Caucasian language
Language: Kabardino-Cherkess
Region: Kabardino-Balkaric ASSR
Capital: Naltshik
Religion: Islam
Christians: unknown
Bible translation: not available

Information:

The Kabardinians have similar ethnic roots as the Adygei people. As early as the 12th to the 14th centuries, an independent nation was founded. In the 16th century, the Kabardinians were integrated to the Russian Empire but they maintained their own national identity. Religion played a significant role in maintaining their independence. Islamic Kabardinians have resisted conversion by Christian missions. Today, there are no known Christians among Kabardinians.

Culturally and politically, the Kabardinians are an isolated minority in their own republic. Despite all attempts of the Soviets to culturally integrate the Kabardinians, national sentiment is growing among them. Mission initiatives in the language and culture of the Kabardinians could bear significant results.

Prayer Concerns:

1. Translate, print, and transport the Bible into the language of the Kabardinians.
2. Awaken missionary interest among many evangelical churches in the area of Kabardino-Balkaric Soviet Republic for the native population.
3. Conversion of intellectual Kabardinians in cities, such as Maikop, Prokhladnii, Baksan, Nartkala and others.
4. Plant churches among the Kabardinians.

4.18 The Adygei (Adyghe)

Population: 109,000
Language group: Caucasian language
Language: Adygei
Region: Adygei Autonomous Area of the RSFSR, Caucasus
Capital: Maikop
Religion: Islam
Christians: none
Bible translation: the Gospel of Mark (1977)

Information:

The Adygei, in the past listed among the Cherkess, are a group which consists of many different Caucasian people groups, such as the Shapsug, Natukhai, Abadzeg, Bzhedug, Temirgoi, and Beslenei. Each of these people groups has a certain ethical self-reliance and independence. They live in the autonomous area of the Adygei in the Krasnodar region, which has a strong concentration of Christian churches.

Probably some of the Adygei have already had some contact with Christians. However, there are no known conversions among the Adygei.

Prayer Concerns:

1. Translate the New Testament into the Adygei language.
2. Print and transport the portions of the Bible that have been translated and any other evangelistic literature available.
3. Awaken an interest in mission among the evangelical Christians in the Krasnodar area for the Adygei.
4. Start evangelistic teams among the youth with a goal to reach the Adygei.
5. Conversion of secularized Adygei in the cities of Krasnodar and Maikop.

4.19 The Abkhaz (Abkhazian)

Population: 91,000
Language group: Caucasian language
Language: Abkhazian
Region: Abkhazian ASSR in the Georgian SSR
Capital: Sukhumi
Religion: Islam
Christians: unknown
Bible translation: Four Gospels (1912); Epistles of John (1981)

Information:

The Abkhazians proudly call their country Apsny ("Land of the Souls") and designate themselves "Apsua" (derived from Apsny). They are the original inhabitants of the Black Sea area and are mentioned for the first time in history as "the nation of Abeshla" in 2nd century B.C. Assyrian documents. This ancient Islamic nation has resisted the influence of their Christian neighbor, the Gruzinians. They are a highly industrialized people group. Cities like Sukhumi, Gagra, Gudauta and others are not only famous tourist centers, but also as industrial and cultural centers. Huge flows of tourists have made the Abkhazians more open to new and different ideas. Even if missionary attempts have appeared not to have had results, the "Land of Souls" is more open than ever before for the Gospel.

Prayer Concerns:

1. Translate the New Testament into the Abkhazian language.
2. Print, transport, and distribute available portions of the Bible.
3. Awaken missionary interest in Georgian and Russian speaking churches in Abkhazian cities for the Abkhazian nation.
4. Conversion of secularized Abkhazians, especially people who are married to a Christian person.
5. Evangelistic contacts by Western tourists with Abkhazian individuals.

4.20 The Cherkess

Population: 46,000
Language group: Caucasian language
Language: Kabardino-Cherkess
Region: northern part of Kabardino-Cherkess Autonomous Area in the RSFSR in the Stavropol Region
Capital: Cherkessk
Religion: Islam
Christians: none
Bible translation: not available

Information:

The name, "Cherkess," is often used to describe several Caucasian people groups. But the Cherkess people group is relatively small in the areas of Stavropol. They are known for their hospitality and friendliness. In the past, they were also known for their fighting and for their brutality.

The Cherkess are strict Muslims. Any Cherkess individual who makes a radical decision against Islam is ostracized from the family. Thus, only a few Cherkess have ever rejected Islam. The agricultural environment makes it difficult to break with tradition and individuals who leave their traditions have a difficult time returning. Christian mission has never been attempted among the Cherkess people.

Prayer Concerns:

1. Translate the New Testament into the Kabardino-Cherkess language.
2. Produce and transport evangelistic literature, slide presentations, and video films for evangelistic purposes to the Cherkess people.
3. Awaken missions interest among Russian, Ukrainian, German, and other evangelical churches in the Stavropol area to the Cherkess people.
4. Conversion of intellectuals among the Cherkess who live in cities.

4.21 The Abaza (Abazin)

Population: 29,000
Language group: Caucasian language
Language: Abasic
Region: northern part of Karachaic-Cherkess Autonomous Area
in the RSFSR; Stavropol Region
Religion: Islam
Christians: none
Bible translation: not available

Information:

The Abazins, related to the Cherkess, represent a minority among the "Cherkess" people group. In the Soviet Union, they are known for their isolated settlements. This isolation resulted from when they moved to their present location during the last century. They have continued to maintain their isolationist position towards other people groups. Mission attempts for the Abazins are unknown.

Prayer Concerns:

1. Translate the New Testament into the Abazic language.
2. Produce and transport evangelistic materials for the Abazins.
3. Awaken mission interest among the evangelical churches in the Stavropol region for the Abazins.
4. Conversion of the few open-minded Abazins in cities.

4.22 The Krysen

Population: several hundred
Language group: Caucasian language
Language: Krysic
Region: northeast Azerbaidzhan SSR.
Cities: the town of Krys in the Kuba region
Religion: Islam/Sunnite
Christians: none
Bible translation: not available

Information:

The Krysen belong to the "Shakhdagic group" of the Lezgin people group, to which the Khinalug also belong. The Khinalug have their own language and today only inhabit one village in the mountains of the Kuba region. The Krysen are cattle breeders. and farming has a subordinate role. In addition to their own language, most Krysen speak Aseri, a trade and written language. Mission attempts are unknown among the Krysen.

Prayer Concerns:

1. Distribute the New Testament in the Aseri language among the Krysen people.
2. Awaken mission interest among Christian churches for the Krysen in the USSR.
3. Start prayer groups for Krysen people.
4. Conversion of intellectual Krysen in cities of Azerbaidzhan.

4.23 The Adzhars

Population: 200,000
Language group: Caucasian language
Language: Georgian (Gruzian)
Region: Adzharic ASSR in the southwestern part of Georgian SSR.
Capital: Batumi
Religion: Islam
Christians: unknown
Bible translation: available

Information:

The Adzhars are related to the Georgians. In the 16th century, the Turks occupied their region and forcefully converted the people to Islam. Only in the period of the Russian-Turkish War (1877-78) did the Adzars free themselves from this occupation. Under the Islamic ruler, the Adzhars Georgians did not change their language but their culture became more Islamic. This led to tensions between their Christian Georgian brothers. Today, however, one may observe an opening of Adzhars towards Georgian influences. An intensive Christian mission for the "fallen" Adzhars was done in the past. Conversion of Adzhars are unknown.

Prayer Concerns:

1. Awaken mission interest among the Georgian Christian churches for their Adzhar brothers.
2. Produce and transport evangelistic video tapes and tracts for Adzhars.
3. Start Christian broadcasts in Georgian with specific messages for the Adzhars.
4. Evangelistic contacts by Western tourists with native individuals.
5. Conversion of open-minded Adzhars and awakening of their historical Christian heritage.

4.24 The Batsbi

Population: several thousand
Language group: Caucasian languages
Language: Batshi/Gruzian
Region: Georgian SSR
Religion: Islam/Sunnite
Christians: unknown
Bible translation: not available

Information:

The Batsbi, also known as the Tsova Tush, are ancestors of the Ingush who came to Gruzia (Georgia) in the 16th century. Here they were subjected to strong assimilation into Georgian culture. Nevertheless, they maintained their ethnic identity and developed their own language. However, their language is no longer used as a trade language. Today, Batshi see themselves more as Georgians.

The assimilation of Batshi with Georgians has influenced the Batshi's religious views. It is not uncommon for Christian Georgians to marry Islamic Batshi. It is believed that a concentrated mission strategy among Batshi would be fruitful.

Prayer Concerns:

1. Awaken mission interest among Christian Georgian churches for the people of Batshi.
2. Conversion of Batshi who are married to Christian partners.
3. Conversion of the intellectual representatives of this people.
4. Conversion of young people who study in universities and have few ties to their people.

4.25 The Bagulal

Population: several hundred
Language group: Caucasian language
Language: Bagulal/Avaric
Region: Dagestan ASSR.
Religion: Islam/Sunnite
Christians: none
Bible translation: not available

Information:

The Bagulals, also called the Kwanadi, primarily live in two regions of the Dagestan ASSR: Zumadin and Achwakh. Culturally and linguistically, the Bagulals are related to the Avars whose written language they also use. However, the Bagulals have kept their traditional and ethnic ties. On the one hand, their own language (Bagulal) is spoken, reflecting their desire to conserve their agrarian traditions but, on the other hand, Avaric serves as their literary language. Most Bugulals work in agriculture and with cattle breeding. Very few have moved to the cities. Mission activities among Bugulals are unknown.

Prayer Concerns:

1. Translate the Bible into the Avaric language.
2. Awaken mission interest among the Caucasian evangelical churches for this people.
3. Conversion of Bagulal youth in schools and cities in Dagestan.

4.26 The Budugh (Budukh)

Population: several hundred
Language group: Caucasian Language
Language: Budukhic
Region: northeastern Azerbaidzhan SSR.
Cities: Kuba, Khatshamas
Religion: Islam/Sunnite
Christians: none
Bible translation: not available

Information:

The Budukh are a small ethnic people group from the Lezgin people group and live in Azerbaidzhan. Most Budukhs know Aseri, their trade and written language, in addition to their own. They are thoroughly integrated with the Aseri people; thus, there are recognizable tendencies that this people group, the Budukh, will disappear in future. The primary activity of the Budukh is cattle breeding and agriculture. Missionary work among the Budukh is unknown.

Prayer Requests:

1. Transport and distribute New Testaments in the Aseri language to the Budukhs.
2. Radio broadcasts in Aseri.
3. Awaken mission interest among Christian churches for the Budukhs and other people groups in Azerbaidzhan.
4. Conversion of influential people among Budukhs.

5. The Turkish Ethnic Groups

The second largest ethnic group is represented by the 24 Turkish groups (more than 16% of the Soviet population). They live scattered throughout the vast regions of European Russia and over practically every Asian region of the Soviet Union. The greatest concentration of the Turkish ethnic groups is found in Central Asia and Siberia.

The European and Central Asian groups belong to the Islamic faith with the exception of the Jewish Karaim. Only a relatively small number of these national groups have accepted the Christian faith. There are "Christian" groups among the Tartars; for example, the Chuvash (or Tavas), the Karachaev, and the Bashkir. The faith of these national groups, originally Christianized by the Russian Orthodox Church, is very weak. Only in isolated instances have members of these groups come to a living faith and become members of Russian-speaking evangelical churches. For these members of the European Turkish language groups, translations of the Bible exist. In contrast, only a small number of translations exist in the languages of the other Central Asian nationalities. However, translation projects are in progress.

Recently, a few of the Uzbeks, Kazaks, and Kirgiz have come to accept the Christian faith. A single case of a Turkman convert has also become known. Other Central Asian nationalities are still completely unreached.

Among the Siberian Turkish nationalities, the Tuvin and the Yakuts are Buddhists. Among the small national minority groups, Shamanistic elements are prevalent. Missionaries of the Orthodox Church attempted to convert the Siberian Turkish nationalities to the Christian faith; however, their efforts were superficial. Today, some Yakuts and Tuvin have become nominal members of the Russian Orthodox Church. In practice, they continue to follow their traditional, cultural beliefs. Instances of evangelical Christians among the Siberian Turkish nationalities are not known.

Mission Concerns:

The Soviet Turkish nationalities represent the greatest challenge for the Christian church in the Soviet Union. Their 50,000,000 members have largely never had any opportunity to hear the message of the gospel.

In the midst of many Turkish national minorities, there are growing evangelical churches. Unfortunately, most of these have only German or Slavic believers without Turkish converts. The German and Slavic believers are in need of being awakened to missionary responsibilities and of seeing the spiritual needs of their Muslim neighbors.

Recently, small groups of German and Russian Christians have begun to take responsibility for their missionary obligation to the Turkish nationalities. They need the prayer support of the congregations in the free world. Even the small groups of converted Christians from these nationalities are beginning to become active among their countrymen. They often do this at risk of their own lives. Christians who are active as missionaries have need of evangelical materials and scriptures in the respective languages of these groups. Christians of the Western world are able to and so are implored to provide assistance.

The situation among the Turkish nationalities in Siberia is quite different. In Siberia, the evangelical churches are primarily located in the urban centers; here, the majority of the population is comprised of immigrants. The natives reside in the sparsely settled rural regions of the taiga. In order to reach these people, Christians will need to be willing to be sent into the vast regions of Siberia as "tent making" missionaries. Recently, some instances of such tent-making ministries have become known. Unfortunately, the home churches of these missionaries do not provide the necessary support. Therefore, it is important that entire congregations be won for the support of the unreached nationalities of Siberia.

Ethnic Overview (Excerpt) of Chapter 5 and 6

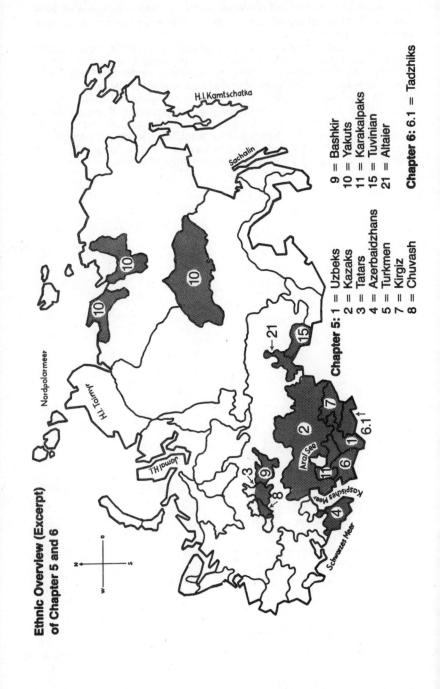

Chapter 5:
1 = Uzbeks
2 = Kazaks
3 = Tatars
4 = Azerbaidzhans
5 = Turkmen
7 = Kirgiz
8 = Chuvash

9 = Bashkir
10 = Yakuts
11 = Karakalpaks
15 = Tuvinian
21 = Altaier

Chapter 6: 6.1 = Tadzhiks

5.1 The Uzbeks

Population: 14,500,000
Language group: Turkish
Language: Uzbek
Region: Uzbekestan (Central Asia)
Capital: Taschbent
Religion: Islam/Sunnite; there are about 50 Christians
Bible translation: Genesis and the Gospel of John (1982)

Information:

The Uzbeks represent one of the largest ethnic groups of the Soviet Union. Their racial origin is mixed. Even today their mixed origins are noticed in the many dialects spoken. The Uzbeks began their ethnic formation at the beginning of the 14th century. Many movements have influenced their culture and religion. Zoroastrianism, Buddhism, and in the early stages even Christianity have left their marks on the Uzbeks' history. Only in the 15th century did the last Christian churches disappear under the pressure of Islam.

The Islamic faith of the Uzbeks is strongly influenced by mysticism and superstition. Politically, culturally, and economically, the Uzbeks are much further advanced than other ethnic groups of Central Asia. If it were possible to win the Uzbeks for Christianity, they could play a decisive role in the evangelization of Central Asia.

Prayer Concerns:

1. Translate the entire Bible into the Uzbek language.
2. Strengthen the small Uzbek congregation in the region of Taschkent.
3. Begin Christian radio broadcasting in the Uzbek language.
4. The conversion of Uzbek leaders and intellectuals.
5. Gain support of Uzbek congregations for the missionary work among the Uzbeks.

5.2 The Kazaks (Kazakhs)

Population: 6,556,000
Language group: Turkish
Language: Kozak
Region: Kazak SSR and bordering areas
Capital: Alma-Ata
Religion: Islam/Sunnite; there are only about 20 Christians
Bible translation: the Gospel of Luke (1983)

Information:

The wide open steppes of Kazakistan have provided refuge for the neighboring ethnic groups of Central Asia for many centuries. In this way, the freedom-loving, yet ever tolerant ethnic group of the Kazaks was formed. Even into the 20th century, they were nomadic. Currently, there are many reminders of their nomadic past in the midst of tremendous industrialization. Only gradually are the rural Kazaks adapting to the pressures of the surrounding modern society. In contrast, a new generation of secular and worldly Kazaks is growing up in the cities.

The official Islamic faith has always played a somewhat lesser role in the life of these people. Therefore, only seldom are the rituals of this religion being practiced. Mosques are found only in a few villages. Their religious practices are determined by animism, although some Kazaks have been Christian for the past few years. Evangelism is carried out intensively in the region of Karaganda and South Kazakistan. Radio broadcasts from Light of the Gospel support this work.

Prayer Concerns:

1 Translate the entire Bible into the Kazak language.
2. Support tent-making missionaries.
3 Form Kazak house fellowships.
4. Broaden the support of the prayer fellowship movement among the Kazaks of the USSR and transfer this prayer support movement to the Western countries.
5 Support Christian radio broadcasts in the Kazak language.

5.3 The Tatars

Population: 6,317,000
Language group: Turkish
Language: Tartar
Region: Tartar SSR along the central portion of the Volga River and in many other regions of the Soviet Union.
Capital: Kasan
Religion: Islam; Christianity/Russian Orthodox
Evangelicals: several thousand
Bible translation: the four gospels and Acts

Information:

The Tartars represent the descendants of Mongolian immigrants from the 13th century. Today, they live in large concentrations in the Tartar SSR, Siberia (the Siberian Tartars), the Caucasus and Central Asia (the Crimean Tartars), and other regions of the Soviet Union. Certain groups display significant differences in language and culture. The Volga Tartars are being especially promoted by the Soviets and their dialect has become the standard for the national spoken and written language.

Several Tartar tribes (e.g. the Nagajbaken and the Krjaschenen) were Christianized between the 16th and 18th centuries; otherwise, Tartars adhere to the Sunnite branch of Islam. In fact, Islam plays only a very secondary role. Several thousand Tartars already belong to evangelical congregations.

Prayer Concerns:

1. Translate the New Testament.
2. Establish Tartar speaking congregations.
3. Start Christian radio broadcasts in the Tartar language.
4. Develop and distribute good, evangelical literature to the Tartars.
5. Begin systematic evangelization efforts among the Tartars.

5.4 The Azerbaidzhans (Azeri Turks)

Population: 5,400,000
Language group: Turkish
Language: Azeri-Turkish
Region: Caucasus
Capital: Baku
Religion: Islam/Shiite
Christians: unknown
Bible translation: the New Testament (1982)

Information:

Originally, the Azerbaidzhans were Christian Georgians, but during the reign of the Arabic Caliphs, from the eighth to the tenth centuries, they converted to Islam. To this day, Islam with all of its traditions and customs is a powerful influence on the Azerbaidzhans in the Soviet republic. Tribal patterns of life patterns are still prevalent and have an especially negative effect on evangelistic efforts. An individual's conversion would definitely result in expulsion from the family and community.

Prevailing circumstances have caused the Azerbaidzhans to become a scattered people. Only 87% live in the Republic; the rest are dispersed throughout the USSR. Some of the Azerbaidzhans who lived in Turkey have settled in Western Europe as foreign workers. If some of these could be reached with the gospel, they could assist in the production of radio broadcasting and evangelical literature.

Prayer Concerns:

1. Distribute the New Testament among the Azerbaidzhan people in the Soviet Union and abroad.
2. Translate the entire Bible into Azeri-Turkish.
3 Awaken missions interest among the evangelical Russian speaking congregations in Azerbaidzhan for the natives.
4. Send Christian missionaries to the Azerbaidzhan.
5. Evangelize the Azerbaidzhans who are living in Western Europe.

Tatar

Azerbaidzhan

Kirgiz

5.5 Smaller people groups from the Azerbaidzhan

Population: several thousand
Language group: Turkish
Language: there are four dialect groups, each with a number of sub-dialects according to region: eastern (Kuba, Baku, and Shemakha dialects), western (Kazak, Gandsha, Karabag, and Airum dialects), northern (Nukha and Zakatalo-Kazak dialects), and southern (Nokhichevan, Erevan, and dialects of Iran)
Region: Azerbaidzhan SSR
Religion: Islam/Shiite
Evangelicals: none
Bible translation: the New Testament in the Azerbaidzhan language

Information:

The Azerbaidzhans are comprised of a number of ethnic groups which, in part, distinguish themselves considerably from one another. The larger groups exist as independent groups (e.g. in Iran). In Azerbaidzhan, there are four main groups: Arjunen, Karapapachen, Padaren, and Shachsewenen. They primarily live in closed communities where their own customs, language, and culture are practiced. The majority are semi-nomadic and are engaged in raising cattle. The young people use the Azerbaidzhan language (Azeri-Turkish) for writing, which is also the main language of the Republic. Slowly the Azerbaidzhan language is replacing the tribal languages in everyday use.

These Muslim ethnic groups of Azerbaidzhan have never heard the Gospel.

Prayer Concerns:

1. Awaken missions interest among the evangelical congregations of the Soviet Union for these smaller ethnic groups.
2 Distribute the New Testament in the Azerbaidzhan language.
3. Conversion of the secular representatives of these people groups who reside in the cities.
4. Send Christian "tent-making" missionaries.

5.6 The Turkmen

Population: 2,028,000 in the U.S.S.R.; additionally, there are 1.35 million in Iran, Afghanistan, and Turkey.
Language group: Turkish
Language: Turkmen; the Oguz division of the Turkic branch of the Uralo-Altaic language family
Region: Turkmen SSR, north of Iran
Religion: Islam/Sunnite
Evangelicals: only one is known
Bible translation: the Gospel of John (1982)

Information:

The Turkmen inhabit mainly the vast sand desert known as the Black Desert. Only a few have changed their partially nomadic lifestyle. Fewer than 10% live in the cities, while the majority work raising cattle and growing cotton.

The Turkmen are Islamic, although their faith is permeated with pagan practices. In large cities, primarily among the young people, atheistic propaganda has brought a noticeable regression in religiosity. However, especially in the interior part of the land, where the greatest amount of the population lives, Islam is very widespread. The result is an anxiety-filled, hopeless life, since Islam, like other pagan-mixed religions, does not offer an optimistic outlook on life.

In the majority of the Turkmen cities, there are no believers. To date, the conversion of only one Turkmen is known. In 1982, the Gospel of John was translated into the Turkmen language and, by 1987, a complete translation of the New Testament was expected.

Prayer Concerns:

1. Awaken missions interest among evangelical congregations in Middle Asia for the Turkmen.
2. Translate the entire Bible into Turkmen.
3. Begin radio broadcasting for the Turkmen.
4. Send Christian missionaries to the Turkmen.

5.7 The Kirgiz (Kirghiz)

Population: 1,906,000
Language group: Turkic
Language: Kirgiz
Region: Kirgiz SSR, west of the Pamir-Altai Mountains
Religion: Islam/Sunnite
Evangelicals: 18 converted and baptized Christians
Bible translation: Acts (1984); Mark and Luke (1987)

Information:

Kirgiztan — "the land of 40 maidens," the common translation among the people. — is a distinct mountainous region; 75% of the 198,500 square km in the territory is higher than 1,500 meters. This is where the Kirgiz live. Kirgiz are a Turkish tribe which arose at the close of the eighth century in the region of the Tienschan.

Their physical appearance reflects Mongolian-like features. They are unusually tall, have dark complexions, high cheek bones, and have small, dark or brown eyes. The inclusion of the Kirgiz into the Soviet Union tore them from their nomadic existence and placed them into "civilized" life. This transition has not been fully accomplished by all the Kirgiz.

In general, there are three Kirgiz tribes which can be categorized according to language, culture, and regions settled. There are many rivalries among them which has often been settled through political channels.

Based upon their religious background, the Kirgiz belong to Islam; however, Islam has never been able to dominate their life. In general, they still cling to many of their traditional practices. During the course of time, an animistic folk-Islam has developed. It is permeated by ancestor worship and demon possession which keeps the people in fear. The continuous atheistic infiltration in the past decades has not removed their fears.

For several years, young Russian and German Christians have made efforts to evangelize the Kirgiz. These young evangelists have encountered opposition, both from the atheistic state as well as from the Islamic leadership. They need a great deal of courage and wisdom. The congregation of the Kirgiz has 18 baptized members.

Prayer Concerns:

1. Praise for the first evangelical missionaries.
2. Translate, print, deliver, and distribute the Bible in the Kirgiz language.
3. Trans-World Radio broadcasts in the Kirgiz language.
4. Develop and deliver good Christian literature.
5. Growth of the first Kirgiz congregation.

5.8 The Chuvash (Tavas)

Population: 1,751,000
Language group: Turkic
Language: Chuvash is the mother tongue of approximately 82% of the population; only about 65% of them know Russian.
Region: the east European part of the Soviet Union, between the Sura and Swijaga Rivers.
Capital: Tcheboksary
Religion: Christian/Russian Orthodox
Evangelicals: several hundred
Bible translation: the Gospel of John (1984)

Information:

Originally, the Chuvash were almost exclusively an agrarian people. At the beginning of this century, only 5% lived in towns. In 1979, about 46% lived in towns and this trend has continued. Abandoning the land can be attributed to the miserable conditions of Soviet agriculture. The urbanization of the Chuvash is accompanied by their secularization.

The sparsely Christianized Chuvash have never had strong ties to Russian Orthodoxy. Consequently, only a few adhere to the church. In addition to an atheistic world-view, a great deal of superstition is also prevalent. Until now, only a few hundred Chuvash have come to believe in the saving power of Jesus Christ.

Prayer Concerns:

1. Translate the entire Bible into the Chuvash language.
2 Print, transport, and distribute the translated Bible sections.
3. Awaken missions consciousness among the evangelical congregations.
4. Begin church planting.
5 Begin evangelical radio broadcasting.

5.9 The Bashkir

Population: 1,371,000
Language group: Turkic
Language: Bashkir
Region: Baschkirian ASSR in the region of the southern Urals.
Capital: Uda
Religion: Islam/Sunnite
Evangelicals: none known
Bible translation: the four gospels (1975)

Information:

The Bashkort (the self-designation of the Bashkir) are Muslim. After centuries of cattle raising, almost overnight they were transported into the industrial age. Today, over 61% of them live in cities. Many of the cities are relatively new and have been established only since the discovery of oil reserves in Baschkirian. The inhabitants of these cities are rootless and, therefore, open to hear the gospel.

Only a very few of the Bashkir still believe in the promises of the communist leaders and there is little understanding of the Islamic confession of faith of their fathers. Many, especially the young, are searching for a meaning in life. Through scripture, they may yet find life's purposes.

Prayer Concerns:

1. Translate the entire New Testament into the Bashkir language.
2. Awaken missions interest among the evangelical congregations of the Bashkir for the native people.
3. Produce, transport, and distribute good, evangelical literature.
4. Begin Christian radio broadcasting.
5. Send missionaries among the Bashkir.

5.10 The Yakuts

Population: 328,000
Language group: Turkic
Language: Yakut
Region: Yakut ASSR in the Valley of Central Lena in eastern Sibera.
Capital: Yakutsk
Religion: 20% Animist; 20% Atheist; 60% nominal Christian
Evangelicals: only a few
Bible translation: the four gospels (1975)

Information:

"Sakha" is the self-designation of the Yakuts. Much of their language, religion, and culture indicates that, from the 10th to the 15th century, the Yakuts wandered in the region around the Baikal Sea and finally settled in the Lena valley. From their earliest beginnings, the Yakuts were cattle and horse breeders. In the 19th century, they learned agriculture from the Russians.

Yakuts are known for their eagerness to learn. Today, they are the most developed tribe among the aborigines of Siberia. Their influence on agriculture, culture, education, and industry is growing steadily. Since 1956, the Yakuts have had a university. One third of the population in the autonomous republic that complete secondary and higher education are Yakuts. They also have the highest percentage of teachers and officials. There are newspapers, books, radio and television programs, films, and dramas in the Yakut language.

During the 18th and 19th century, most of the Yakuts were Christianized by Russian Orthodox missionaries. In contrast to other Siberian tribes, the mission efforts caused the traditional animistic religion to lose much of its influence. However, only a few Yakuts have experienced a living faith in Christ. There are no evangelical churches.

Prayer Concerns:

1. Translate the Bible into the Yakut language.
2. Print, transport, and distribute the existing gospels.
3. Awaken missions interest among congregations of Siberia for the Yakut.
4. Send missionaries to the Yakut.
5. Establish a church in Yakutsk.
6. Conversion of Orthodox priests who work with the Yakut.
7. Develop, transport, and distribute evangelical books and tracts in the Yakut language.
8. Begin radio broadcasts for the Yakut.

Chuvash

Yakut

Tuvinian

5.11 The Karakalpaks

Population: 303,000
Language group: Turkic
Language: Karakalpak
Region: the Karakalpak ASS in the Uzbek SSR (south of the Aral Sea) and bordering regions.
Capital: Nukus
Religion: Islam
Evangelicals: none
Bible translation: not available

Information:

The Karakalpaks emerged through the process of integration of native inhabitants of the region with invaders, such as the Grumms, Turks, Nagiers, and others. Toward the end of the 18th century, the current language of the Karakalpaks was essentially developed. Under the rule of the Uzbek Khans, the Karakalpaks remained culturally underdeveloped. In the course of the last decade, the Soviets made this nomadic group of people a self-reliant nation. Accompanying modernization, these desert inhabitants have shown a noticeable increase in secularization.

Folk-Islam, a mixture of traditional Islamic conceptions with animistic ancestor worship, is practiced by the rural population. However, the younger generation of Karakalpaks is searching for a better way of life. Marxism has been unable to provide what was promised.

Prayer Requests:

1. Translate the New Testament into the Karakalpak language.
2. Awaken a mission consciousness among the Christians of Uzbekistan for the Karakalpaks.
3. Send Christian missionaries into the regions of Karakalpak which are being quickly industrialized.
4. Conversion of influential men in the capital city of Nukus.

5.12 The Kumyk

Population: 228,000
Language group: Turkic
Language: Kumyk
Region: the northern part of Dagestan SSR
Religion: Islam/Sunnite
Evangelicals: none
Bible translation: the Gospels of Matthew and Mark (1897)

Information:

The Kumyk people formed as a result of intermarriage between the aborigines of Dagestan and Turkic speaking tribes, such as the Kypchak. Among the Kumyk, one can distinguish three distinct ethnic groups: the Khasa, Buinak, and Kaitak. Today, their differences are disappearing.

The Kumyk are farmers and live in communes in the northern Agestanistanian plains. The younger Kumyk are moving to more urban areas where they are breaking with the traditions of their elders and with Islam. There is no knowledge of Christian missions among the Kumyk.

Prayer Requests:

1. Translate the New Testament into the Kumyk language.
2. Awaken mission interest among the Christian churches of the USSR for the Kumyk.
3 Establish groups to prayerfully support evangelism among the Kumyk.
4. Begin a mission project among both the Kumyk students and intellectuals in the cities.
5. Develop and distribute Christian videos in the Kumyk language.

5.13 The Uighurs (Uigurs)

Population: 211,000
Language group: Turkic
Language: Uiguric
Region: Kazak, Uzbeck, and Kirgiz SSR
Religion: Islam/Sunnite
Evangelicals: none
Bible translation: the Gospel of Mark (1982), New Testament (1986)

Information:

In the 19th century, due to political unrest, the Uigurs came from China to the Soviet region of Central Asia. To this day, the Uigurs are scattered throughout colonies in most regions of Central Asia. In many regions, there has been frequent intermarriage among the Uigurs, Uzbecks, and Kirgizians. A strong ethnic identity has developed among the Uigurs in the regions of Alma-Ata, Taldy-Kurgan, and Fergana.

Like most people in Central Asia, the Uigurs work in agriculture and cattle breeding. Active Christian churches were recorded among the Uigurs until the 15th century. Later, Islam gained influential power. Today there are no known Christians among the Uigurs.

Prayer Requests:

1. Translate the New Testament into the Uiguric language.
2. Awaken mission interest among congregations of Central Asia for the Uigurs.
3. Begin mission activity among the Uigurs in the urban centers.
4. Conversion of young Uigurs in the cities.
5. Develop and distribute Christian tracts and videos among the Uigurs.

5.14 The Gagauz

Population: 173,000
Language group: Turkic
Language: Gagauz
Region: southern part of the Moldavian SSR (Bessarabia) and scattered on the bordering regions of the Ukraine.
Religion: Christianity/Russian Orthodox
Evangelicals: unknown
Bible translation: the Gospel of Matthew

Information:

The Gagauz did not come from Bulgaria into the Russian Empire until the l9th century. Their precise origin cannot be determined. Possibly, they may have been Turks who originally converted to the Christian faith and accepted Slavic influence. Today, they represent a distinct group of people who live scattered among the Moldavians and the Ukrainians. They work in agriculture.

The few Christians among the Gagauz belong to the Moldavian, Ukrainian, and Russian congregations.

Prayer Requests:

1. Translate the New Testament into the Gagauz language.
2 Awaken mission interest among the believing Gagauz for their own people.
3 Establish Gagauzic speaking congregations.
4. Initiate mission efforts among believers of other language speakers for the Gagauz.
5 Conversion of the Gagauzic speaking Orthodox clergy.

5.15 The Tuvinian

Population: 166,000
Language group: Turkic
Language: Tuvinian
Region: the Turvinian ASSR in South Siberia
Capital: Kyzl
Religion: Buddhism
Evangelicals: none
Bible translation: not available

Information:

The Tuvinian live in a land of extreme climatic variation; sizzling hot summers merge with ice-cold winters. It is also a land of geographic contrasts; high mountains descend into steppes and deserts.

The Tuvinian are hunters and breed both cattle and horses. During their long history, the Tuvinian have been ruled by various peoples. For centuries, they were controlled by Mongolians and Chinese. In 1944, the then-independent Peoples Republic of Tannu-Tuva, in the RSFSR, was admitted as an autonomous Tuvin Region. In 1961, this region became an ASSR. This had significant consequences, especially with respect to their religion.

The Tuvinian are Lamaistic Buddhists, although Shamanistic beliefs are also prevalent. Prior to their admission to the Soviet Union, there were numerous monasteries; however, most of them had to relinquish their property to the State. Robbed of their culture, tradition, and religion, the Tuvinian have become open to the gospel.

Prayer Requests:

1. Awaken mission interest among the evangelical congregations of Siberia and the rest of the Soviet Union for the Tuvinian.
2. Translate the scriptures into the Tuvinian language.
3. Send missionaries to the Tuvinian.
4. Conversion of intellectual Tuvinian; e.g., students in the large cities.

5.16 The Karachai (Karachaev)

Population: 131,000
Language group: Turkic
Language: Karachai-Balkar
Region: the Southern part of the Karachai-Cherkessk Autonomous
Region of the RSFSR in the region of the Caucasus.
Capital: Karachaevsk-Cherkessk
Religion: Islam/Sunnite
Evangelicals: none
Bible translation: the Gospel of Mark (1978)

Information:

The ancestors of the "Karachaili," as the Karachai call themselves, comprise the original settlers of today's Karachai-Cherkessk Autonomous Region. The Karachai tribe was developed through intermarriage with other groups in the region and with Turkic speaking immigrants.

Since 1936, the Karachai have had their own written language known as Balkar. In Karachaevsk, there is a teacher education institution which is responsible for the intellectual development of future generations. In contrast to the other smaller Caucasian groups, the Karachai are more outgoing, a trait which has contributed to the secularization among this Islamic people.

Toward the end of the 19th century, the Orthodox church attempted to Christianize the Karachai. The attempt was without success. Today, Christian missionaries would probably have more fruitful results.

Prayer Requests:

1. Translate the New Testament into the Karachai-Balkar language.
2. Awaken missions interest among Christian congregations in the Caucasus for the Karachai people.
3. Establish groups to pray for evangelism among the Karachai.
4. Conversion of Karachai in mixed marriages who have broken ties with family and traditional religion.

5.17 The Turks

Population: 93,000
Language group: Turkic
Language: Turkish
Region: the Republics of Central Asia and the Caucasus
Religion: Islam/Sunnite
Evangelicals: unknown
Bible translation: available

Information:

The Turks represent, in part, the remains of the oldest Turkish inhabitants of middle Asia. Most of the Turks left middle Asia during the 11th-13th centuries; nevertheless, Turkish settlements continued to exist in their old home. As a result of Turkish conquests, the Caucasian Turks settled in the Caucasus.

Today, the Turks often live in cities where they work as merchants. Only a few remain in rural areas. Missionaries have never reached out to the Soviet Turks.

Prayer Requests:

1. Transport and distribute Turkish Bibles to the Soviet Union.
2. Awaken missions interest among evangelical congregations of the southern Soviet Union for the Turkish people.
3. Conversion of secularized Turks in the cities.
4. Establish missionary house fellowships among the Turks.
5. Transport evangelical literature and videos in the Turkish language to the Soviet Union.

5.18 The Khakass

Population: 71,000
Language group: Turkic
Language: Kacha (Khaas)
Region: the Khakass Autonomous Region south of Krisnojarsk
Capital: Ababan
Religion: Animism
Evangelicals: unknown
Bible translation: not available

Information:

Khakass is the name ascribed to five Turkish tribes: Kacha, Kyzyl, Sagai, Beltir, and Koibal. Today, these earlier nomads have been gathered into communes and have entered the occupation of sheep, goat, cattle, and horse raising.

Many of the Khakass have completely removed themselves from agriculture occupations and have integrated into the life of industrialization. In this transition, a great change has taken place among the tribes. As always in such changes, a great deal of their original world-view has been lost.

The Khakasses are animists. In order to ward off bad-luck and ensure good harvests, they make pictures of spirits. However, the process of industrialization has decreased the importance of their traditional animistic faith. Still, the Marxist, atheistic world-view is essentially foreign to their way of life. Christian missions could have a good opportunity to bring the good news of salvation.

Prayer Requests:

1. Awaken missions interest among evangelical congregations in southern Siberia for the Khakass.
2. Conversion of the Khakasses living in cities.
3. Translate, publish, transport, and distribute good Christian tracts as well as portions of the New Testament.
4. Send Christian missionaries into the region of the Khakass.

5.19 The Balkars

Population: 66,000
Language group: Caucasian Language
Language: Karachai-Balkar
Region: Kabardino-Balkaric ASSR in the northern Caucasus
Capital: Naltshik
Religion: Islam
Christians: none
Bible translation: not available

Information:

The Balkarian people group may be traced to some North Caucasian tribes who integrated with the Balkars and the Kypchak Turks during the 12th century. Under pressure from the Mongols, the Balkars moved to the mountains. Here, in the valleys of the Caucasus mountains, they retained their independence until the last century. Integration with the Russian Empire, and later into the Soviet Union, did not change the life style of this Islamic people. In fact, they are still isolated from other people groups. Missionary endeavors among the Balkars are unknown.

Prayer Concerns:

1. Translation of the Bible into the language of the Balkars and the transport and distribution of parts of the Bible.
2. Awaken mission interest in the Christian churches in Balkaria for the native people.
3. Start mission work among urban Balkars and pray for the conversion of intellectual Balkars.
4. Start prayer groups in the Russian speaking churches in Balkaria with a goal of reaching the native population.

5.20 The Nogai

Population: 60,000
Language group: Turkish language
Language: Nogaic
Region: the Nogaic steep in the Stavropol Region and in the Dagestan ASSR (Caucasus)
Religion: Islam/Sunnite
Christians: unknown
Bible translation: the Four Gospels (1925)

Information:

The Nogaic people are descendants from different Turkish and Mongolian tribes which intermarried during the time of Mongolian rule. The Turkish language was adopted. Today, there are three different groups of Nogaic people: the Ak, Achikulak, and the Kara Nogai. The differences among them are minor, however.

The majority of these former nomads work in agriculture and cattle breeding. Only a few Nogai live the traditional nomadic life because it is not tolerated by the Soviet State.

Prayer Concerns:

1. Translate portions of the New Testament into the language of the Nogai.
2. Awaken missionary interest among Christians in the Stavropol region for the Nogaic people.
3. Start prayer groups for the evangelization of the Nogai.
4. Conversion of the intellectuals. Conversion of Nogaic students in the Soviet cities.

5.21 The Altai

Population: 60,000
Language group: Turkish language
Language: Altaic
Region: Gorno-Altaic Autonomous Region, South Siberia, along the border to China and Mongolia.
Capital: Gorno-Altaisk
Religion: 98% Animists; 2% Atheists
Christians: none
Bible translation: the Four Gospels (1975)

Information:

The majority of the Altai people live in the Gorno-Altaic Autonomous Region in South Siberia. They actually represent a group of smaller people groups but, since the Soviet reign, they are considered one nation. The Tubalars, Chelkans, and Kumandins live in the north of the Altai region; the Telengit, Telesy, and Teleut live in the south. Approximately half of the Altai people speak Russian; but, 87% regard the Altaic language as their mother language. Most Altai people live in the country as cattle breeders and agriculture workers; in the mountains, they are hunters.

Their lifestyle has changed little over the past centuries. In their Shamanistic rituals they worship Ulgen, the spirit of heaven, or the Erlik, the spirit of the underworld. Their religion is characterized by fear and belief in demons. Only a few Altai have turned to atheism. Christians among them are unknown.

Prayer Concerns:

1. Translation of the Bible into the language of Altai people.
2. Awakening missionary interest in the Christian churches in Siberia for the Altai people.
3. Publication, transportation, and distribution of existing translated portions of the New Testament.
4. Sending the first missionaries to the Altai people.
5. Mission efforts for the Russian speaking Altai people.

5.22 The Shors

Population: 16,000
Language group: Turkish language
Language: Shoric
Region: Kusnezk Alatau, along the Tom river (southern Siberia)
Religion: animists
Christians: none
Bible translation: not available

Information:

The mountainous region where the Shors live is a famous industrial area in the Soviet Union, the Kussbass (Kusnezk coal mines). Until the 17th century, the Shors were iron-workers; today, the majority of Shors work on collective farms. They are noted for their hunting and fishing.

The Shors are animists. They not only believe in the spirits of animals, mountains, and forests, they also worship these spirits. Generally, those who work in the Kussbass Industrial Complex lose their connection to the land and to their religion.

Prayer Concerns:

1. Awakening missionary interest in many evangelical Christians who live as neighbors with the Shors.
2. Sending a missionary to the area where Shors live.
3. Distributing good evangelical literature among the younger Shors.
4. Conversion of intellectual Shors, who would be capable of evangelizing their people.

5.23 The Dolgans

Population: 5,100
Language group: Turkish language
Language: Yakut
Region: Autonomous Region Taimyr on the Taimyr Peninsula in northern Siberia.
Religion: nominal Orthodox Christians; Shamanists
Christians: none
Bible translation: the Four Gospels (1975)

Information:

The Dolgans are one of the youngest people groups in the Soviet Union. They emerged as a distinct people group during the last century through integration of Evenks, Yakuts, and Russian settlers. The Dolgans speak a Dolganic dialect of the Yakut language. Their religion is a mixture of Shamanistic and Christian beliefs.

Prayer Concerns:

1. Awakening missionary interest among the Soviet churches for the Dolgan.
2. Conversion of Russian Orthodox priests who serve among the Dolgan.
3. Sending a missionary to the Dolgan.
4. Publishing, transporting, and distributing the existing four gospels in the Yakut language for the Dolgan.

5.24 The Karaims

Population: 3,300 (1979)
Language group: Turkish language
Language: Karaimic
Region: Crimea, Ukraine, and Lithuania; a small group lives in Poland
Religion: Judaism
Christians: unknown
Bible translation: not available

Information:

The Karaims are descendants of Turkish tribes which formed the Khazaric Kingdom. Today, most of the Karaims live in Crimea. There are almost no contacts among the various groups of Karaims. They developed discernable differences in their languages. In the Ukraine, and especially in Lithuania and Poland, the Karaims have almost completely integrated into the native cultures.

Missionary endeavors among Karaims are unknown. They could be reached by the Gospel from the native people of the areas in which they live. An exception could be the Crimea-Karaims who have a stronger ethnic identity.

Prayer Concerns:

1. Awakening missionary interest among the native evangelical Christians for their Karaim neighbors.
2. Conversion of leading individuals among Karaims.
3. Founding evangelistic home groups among the Karaims.
4. Responsible prayer partnership from Christians in the West or East for the Karaim people.

5.25 The Tofalars (Karagass)

Population: 800-1000
Language group: Turkish language
Language: Tofa
Region: northeast of the Sayan Mountains and along the Uda, Ija, and other small Ob rivers (south-central Siberia)
Religion: animism
Christians: none
Bible translation: not available

Information:

The Tofalars live on collective farms and work in cattle breeding. They enjoy bear, deer, and sable hunting. The women pick wild berries to supplement food supplies. The religious beliefs of the Tofalars is dominated by fear of spirits. Their priests (shamans) make sacrifices to satisfy the spirits in order to be successful in hunting.

Prayer Concerns:

1. Awakening mission interest among evangelical churches in Western Siberia for the Tofalars.
2. Conversion of intellectual Tofalars.
3. Sending a missionary to the Tofalars.

5.26 The Mishars

Population: unknown
Language group: Turkish language
Language: Tatar
Region: central region of the Volga river in the Tatar ASSR
Religion: Islam
Christians: unknown
Bible translation: not available

Information:

Ethnically, the Mishars belong to the Volga Tatars, but they are substantially different from them. In Bashkiria, they are called "Mishcheryak" and "Tatars," which could imply a link to a Finno-Ugrian language group. Like the Volga Tatars, the Mishars speak the Tatar language. The majority live in the country, but some have already moved to the cities. It is unknown if there are Christian Mishars.

Prayer Concerns:

1. Translating the whole Bible into the Tatar language.
2. Starting Christian radio broadcasts in Tatar with special messages for the Mishars.
3. Awakening mission interest among the evangelical churches in that region for the Mishar people.
4. Founding Christian home groups for the Mishars.

5.27 The Kreshen (Kryashen)

Population: unknown
Language group: Turkish language
Language: Tatar
Region: Tatar ASSR (middle Volga)
Religion: Christianity/Russian Orthodox
Christians: several hundred
Bible translation: not available

Information:

The Kreshen are related to the Islamic Kazan Tatars. From the 16th to 18th centuries, the Russian Orthodox Church forced the Kreshen to become Christians. Their new religion separated them from their Islamic brothers and they have developed their own culture and dialect.

Today, the Kreshen live in cities as well as in the country. Their relationship to the Orthodox Church is for the most part unclear. Superstition prevails in many places but it is especially strong in rural areas. Only a few Kreshen have become Christians.

Prayer Concerns:

1. Translating the whole Bible into the Tatar language. Transporting existing literature to that region.
2. Awakening mission interest among believing Kreshen for their people.
3. Starting Christian radio broadcasts in the Tatar language.
4. Founding home groups and churches among the Kreshen.

5.28 The Nagaibak (Noghaibaq)

Population: unknown
Language group: Turkish language
Language: Nagaibak, Tatar
Region: Bashkirian ASSR, Tshelyabinsk region (southern Ural Mountains)
Religion: Christianity/Russian Orthodox
Christians: unknown
Bible translation: not available

Information:

The Nabaibak are probably descendants of the so-called Mongolian Tatars who settled along the Ik river (a tributary of the Kama). In the 16th century, they were forcefully Christianized and their commitment to the Christian religion never deeply rooted. Old pagan influences are still alive today.

The Nabaibak work in agriculture and cattle breeding. Only a few live in cities.

Unlike the policy toward other small people groups, the Soviet government has neglected the Nagaibaks and declared them to be only a dialect group of the Tatars. Although the government neglects other ethnic groups, it at least recognizes their existence.

Prayer Concerns:

1. Awakening mission interest among churches of that region for the Nagaibak.
2. Sending Tatar believers as missionaries to the Nagaibak.
3. Conversion of the Russian Orthodox priests who serve among Nagaibak.
4. Founding Christian home groups and churches for the Nagaibak.

5.29 Beserman (Besermyan)

Population: about 50,000
Language group: Turkish language
Language: Besermanic/Udmurtic
Region: northern part of the Udmurtic ASSR
Religion: Christianity/Greek Orthodox
Christians: unknown
Bible translation: not available

Information:

Today, the Beserman are regarded as Udmurts, although there are major cultural and language differences. They are seen as direct descendants of the Volga Bulgarians and have a rich cultural past. Through a process of assimilation with the Udmurts, the Beserman have tended to loose their cultural identity.

The majority of the Beserman work in agriculture. Although they have belonged to the Orthodox Church for many centuries, they do not know the Word of God or the basic truth of Christianity. Many have left the church.

Prayer Concerns:

1. Awakening mission interest among the evangelical churches in that region for the Beserman people.
2. Conversion of orthodox priests.
3. Translating the Bible in the Udmurt language and distributing existing parts of the Bible among the Beserman.
4. Sending missionaries to the region of the Beserman people.

6. The Iranians

The Iranians are extolled as the wisest people in the Orient. This group includes the Tadzhik, a very friendly people who live on the outskirts of South Central Asia. The Tadzhik belong to the Iranian part of the Indo-European language group.

Within the Soviet Union live twelve tribes of Iranians with cumulative population of 4,177,000. Of these tribes, only the Ossetian, Tat, Tadzhik, and other small tribes still live in their ancestral territories. The others represent immigrants from the neighboring regions of Turkey, Iran, Afghanistan and Pakistan. Virtually, since the turn of the century, the Iranians have lived in what is now the modern Soviet Union.

With the exception of a few Tats and Ossetians, who belong to the Jewish or Christian religions, the Iranians consider themselves Islamic.

For the most part, an attempt has not been made to convert these people to Christianity. In the most widely-used languages, translations of portions of the Bible exist.

Mission Concerns:

The majority of the Iranian people live in areas that have a strong concentration of German and Russian evangelical communities. Unfortunately, these evangelical groups have not yet discovered the open mission field which stands before their door.

The few missionary-inclined Christians lack the knowledge as well as the means by which to reach their neighbors. They need the prayer support of brothers and sisters in the West and also their material help for the publication of printed works and tracts as well as other evangelical material in the language of the Iranian people.

6.1 The Tadzhiks

Population: 2,898,000
Language group: Iranian language
Language: Tadzhik
Region: Tadzhik SSR, northeastern Afghanistan
Capital: Duschanbe
Religion: Islam/Sunnite
Christians: only a few
Bible translations: New Testament (1983)

Information:

"The roof of the world" is what one calls Tadzhik SSR. Here, in a barely accessible mountainous region, live the Tadzhiks. Altogether, there are about 9.15 million Tadzhiks in the world (primarily in Afghanistan). They are Sunnite and are famous for their wisdom. Their conception of religion is strongly influenced by Buddhism and Zoroastrianism, which are still alive today within the popular Islamic devotion.

Even though missionaries came to the Tadzhik very early (5A.D.), the tribe received a translation of the New Testament for the first time in 1983. Interest in the translations is especially great among the secular Tadzhik who live in the cities. However, less than five Tadzhiks have come to believe in Jesus Christ.

Prayer Concerns:

1. Awaken mission interest for the Tadzhik among the Russian and German churches of Tadzhikistan.
2. Publish, transport, and distribute Tadzhik New Testaments.
3. Pray that the few believers will be granted the courage to witness and the power to proclaim the gospel for the Lord.
4. Translate and distribute good evangelical tracts in Tadzhik.
5. Convert Tadzhik refugees in Pakistan.
6. Begin radio work in the Tadzhik language.

Tadzhik

6.2 The People of the Pamir

Population: a few thousand
Language group: Iranian
Language: Tadzhik
Region: Pamir mountains in the eastern part of the Tadzhik SSR
Religion: Islam; animists
Christians: none
Bible translations: the Tadzhik New Testament

Information:

The often inaccessible valleys of the Pamir mountains have greatly contributed to the formation of groups of people very different from each other. Many of these tribes have only a few hundred inhabitants. In contrast, other tribes are so large that the government has given them their own autonomous regions, such as the Gorno-Badakhshan Autonomous Region. Here live the Yazgulem, Rushan, Bartang, Oroshor, Shugnan, Badzhui, Ishkashim, and Wakhan. The Yagnob live on the highest tier of the Serawschan River (Turkestan mountain chain, west of the Pamir) and are descendants of the related tribe, the Sogdier.

Today one finds a gradual integration of these people into the Tadzhik nation. Tadzhik is the main written and spoken language.

In spite of an intensive attempt at integration into the state, the Pamir people nevertheless remain, thanks to their geographic surroundings, isolated from the rest of the world.

Prayer Concerns:

1. Awakening missionary interest among the churches of Tadzhik SSR for the people of Pamir.
2. Distribute the Tadzhik New Testament to the Pamir by way of Christian mountaineers, geologists, and workers for the energy complexes of Serawschan.
3 Conscientious broadcasting by some missionaries in the Pamir mountain region.
4. Begin Christian broadcasting of the Tadzhik language.
5. Convert representatives of the various tribes who are studying in Tadzhik cities.

6.3 The Ossetian

Population: 542,000
Language group: Iranian language
Language: Ossetian
Region: North Ossetian ASSR; South Ossetian Autonomous Region of the Georgian SSR and Georgian SSR (Caucasus)
Cities: Ordschenikidse, Zchinwali
Religion: Islam
Christians: a few hundred
Bible translations: the Gospel of John (1984)

Information:

The "Iron" — as the Ossetian call themselves — are an old, Caucasian civilized nation. Their mobile and centuries-long history reveals the trails of many immigrants and conquerors. Since Russia's annexation of the North in 1774 (the South remained in the Gruzian empire), the Ossetians have been divided into two groups to this day. They differ according to openness to the world; the North is open while the South remains secluded and closed to innovation. Life in the mountainous South probably also played a role in their value of privacy. The "progressiveness" of the North is reflected in the high divorce rate (14.9) and the high number of urban dwellers (71%).

In the 1920s, in North Ossetian, missions had been carried out by Christian evangelicals. Through their efforts a small church, which still exists today, came into being. The Christians of Ossetian have a deep longing to reach their people for Christ.

Prayer Concerns:

1. Print and distribute the New Testament in the Ossetian language.
2. Strengthen and train Ossetian believers for mission to their countrymen.
3. Grounding of prayer circles in the West for the support of this mission.
4. Grounding of a Christian Bible study group in the small cities in North and South Ossetian.

6.4 The Kurds

Population: 116,000
Language group: Iranian
Language: Kurdish
Region: Armenia, Azerbaidzhan, and Georgian SSR; a small group lives in the Turkmen SSR.
Religion: Islam; Sunnite, Jesid, and Shiite
Christians: none
Bible translations: not available

Information:

The Kurds (who call themselves Kurmandzh) moved from Turkey and settled in the Caucasus at the turn of the century. One reason for this emigration was that the majority of Kurds who had settled in Armenia were members of the Jesid sect of Islam and they were being persecuted in Turkey.

The Soviet Union has continually supported the Kurds national consciousness; for example, they supported the development of an alphabet based upon Cyrillic. The Soviets are pleased to point out to neighboring countries that they help the Kurdish minorities. But in spite of these assertions, the Kurds do not have a homeland nor have they been reached by the Gospel of Christ.

Most Kurds work in agriculture. In Gruzinian, where more Kurds live in the cities, they work in industry.

Prayer Concerns:

1. Translate the Holy Scriptures into the Kurdish language.
2. Awakening of mission interest in the East and the West for the Kurds who have been dispersed throughout the Soviet Union and the world.
3. Convert Kurds in the West, particularly West Germany.
4. Convert secular Kurds in the cities of Georgia.

6.5 The Persians

Population: 31,000
Language group: Iranian language
Language: Persian
Region: in and around the cities of Samarkand and Buchara (Uzbek SSR)
Religion: Islam/Shiite
Christians: none
Bible translations: not available

Information:

The Soviet Persians are descendants of a well-to-do class of the Middle-Asian Emirate. They came as businessmen, artists, and scientists to Samarkand and Buchara. The first Christian missionaries, who came in the 5th or 6th century A.D., were Persian.

Today, the Persians have a subordinate role. Massive efforts to assimilate them has resulted in the younger generation identifying more and more with the Uzbeks (in Samarkand) or Tadzhiks (in Buchara). Due to this assimilation, the two languages are used for both written and oral communication.

Because the Persians represent a Shiite minority within a Sunni majority of Uzbeks and Tadzhiks, they have maintained a strong religious self-awareness.

Prayer Concerns:

1. Awaken mission consciousness among the churches of the Central Asian cities.
2. Transport Persian New Testaments to Samarkand and Buchara.
3. Convert Persian intellectuals and establish a mission team in Samarkand or Buchara.
4. Transmit Christian radio broadcasts in Persian for the Soviet population.

6.6 The Tats

Population: 22,000
Language group: Iranian
Language: Tat
Region: northeastern Azerbaidzhan SSR
Religion: Islam, Judaism, Christianity (Monophysite)
Evangelicals: unknown
Bible translation: not available

Information:

In terms of religion, the Tats represent one of the most interesting people of the Caucasus. They divide themselves into three different religious groups: the Shiite Tats are Islamic, the mountain dwellers are Jewish, and another group are Monophysite Christians. Although religious boundaries cross one another, this small group of Tats have maintained a common language.

The Jewish Tats are occupied in cattle-breeding and horticulture, while the Islamic and Christian Tats work more in agriculture and industry.

Prayer Concerns:

1. Awaken mission interest among Soviet Christians for the Tats. Send Christian missionaries into the Tat villages.
2. Convert Islamic and Jewish Tats and plant an evangelical church among them.
3. The conversion of Orthodox priests.
4. Distribute Christian literature among the Tats.

6.7 The Beluchi (Baluch)

Population: unknown
Language group: Iranian language
Language: Beluchi
Region: the district of Mari in the Turkmen SSR and in the southern part of Tadzhik SSR
Religion: Islam
Christians: none
Bible translations: not available

Information:

The Beluchi primarily live in Pakistan. A small group, in the course of the past century, have settled in Central Asia. There, in spite of the disrupted contact with their homeland, they have maintained their ethnic and linguistic distinctions.

The Beluchi essentially live off the land; often in ethnically self-contained settlements. In South Tadzhik SSR, the Beluchi have integrated with a small group of the Bragner. The Beluchi work in agriculture and cattle-breeding. Both the Turkmen and the Tadzhik languages are used for writing.

Missionary endeavors among the Beluchi are unknown.

Prayer Concerns:

1. Translate the Bible into the language of the Beluchi; transport and distribute the Bible among the Soviet Beluchi.
2. Awaken mission interest among the Central Asian churches for the Beluchi and the people of the Bragner.
3. Convert secular Beluchi in the cities.
4. Establish prayer groups for the support of missions to the Beluchi in the USSR and other Asian countries.

6.8 The Talysh (Talush)

Population: unknown
Language group: Iranian
Language: Talush
Region: southeastern part of Azerbaidzhan SSR
Religion: Islam
Christians: none
Bible translation: not available

Information:

Outside of Azerbaidzhan, the Talysh (self-designated the "Talush") live in the neighboring territory of Iran. In the USSR, one can observe an increasing integration of the Talysh and the Aseri; a common culture and language bind them together.

The majority of the Talysh still live in the country where most are active in cattle-breeding.

Through the assimilation of the rural Azerbaidzhan, some tribal traditions are being lost. At the same time, individuals who succeed in moving to the city do not, all at once, lose complete contact with their clan.

Prayer Concerns:

1. Awaken mission interest among the Christians in the USSR for the Talysh.
2. Transport and distribute the New Testament in the Aseri language for the more open Talysh in the large cities. Convert influential personalities.
3. Start prayer groups in both the East and the West for the evangelization of the Talysh.
4. Develop and transport Christian video films in Aseri for use among the Talysh.

7. The Finno-Ugrian Peoples

The native home of the Finno-Ugrian people is the Ural Mountains. At the present time, 17 groups within this larger Finno-Ugrian group live in the Soviet Union with a total population of 4,436,000. Because of their different history, the Finno-Ugrian live throughout the Soviet Union and have adopted different cultures.

On the one hand, the Estonians, Finns, and Hungarians belong to the European culture; on the other, the Vogul (Mansi) and Khant (Ostyak) have a primitive culture. Still others within the Finno-Ugrian group have adopted the Russian culture.

All Finno-Ugrian peoples have been confronted with the gospel in some way or another. The Estonians, Finns, and Hungarians have their national churches. The Estonians and Finns are strongly represented in the Evangelical-Lutheran churches; the Hungarians belong to either the Reformed or the Roman-Catholic church. Among some of these churches we find living, evangelical congregations. This is particularly true in Estonia where many Baptist, Methodist, and Pentecostal churches exist.

The Mordvin, Mari, Udmurt, Karyalen, Veps, Izhor, and a few Zyryan were missionized by the Russian Orthodox Church. Among them we can find evangelical Christians. National (native) churches are not known to us.

As with the previous nations, the Russian Orthodox Church missionized the Finno-Ugrian population as well. Unfortunately, the Word did not make deep roots. Pagan thinking is still widespread among this population.

Mission Request:

Although some nations have big evangelical churches, many people have never heard the good news. Bible translations exist only in a few of these languages. Even nominal Orthodox Christians live in the evil of paganism.

The evangelicals of the Soviet Union have done very little missionizing among the culturally distinct Finno-Ugrian groups. Christians have tended not to take responsibility for the cross-cultural mission. Even the Finno-Ugrian evangelicals fail to see their own people as part of the mission field.

In order to do mission among the unreached Finno-Ugrian people, the native Christians must take missionary responsibility. The native Christians should be the primary missionaries. Christians from the West can only give them a hand. This "helping hand" is very important.

Ethnic Overview (excerpt) of Chapter 7 and 8

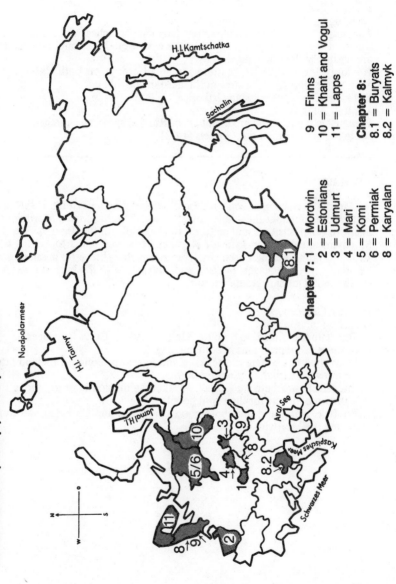

Chapter 7:
1 = Mordvin
2 = Estonians
3 = Udmurt
4 = Mari
5 = Komi
6 = Permiak
8 = Karyalan

9 = Finns
10 = Khant and Vogul
11 = Lapps

Chapter 8:
8.1 = Buryats
8.2 = Kalmyk

7.1 The Mordvin (Mordvinian)

Population: 1.2 million; approximately 1/3 live in Mordvin ASSR, south of Gorki
Language group: Finno-Ugrian languages
Language: the Mordvin belong to two language branches; Moksha is found in the west, Erzya is found in the east. Both books and newspapers are written in both languages.
Region: Mordvin ASSR, scattered in small groups on both sides of the Volga River (north of Saratow in Kazakistan and Siberia).
Religion: Christians/Russian Orthodox
Capital: Saransk
Evangelicals: a few who are members of Russian speaking churches
Bible translation: the Four Gospels (1973)

Information:

Mordvins, in comparison with the other small nations of the USSR, are scattered throughout the whole Soviet Union. This has forced Mordvins to adapt to other customs and cultures. For example, in the Tatar ASSR, the Mordvins speak either Tatar or Russian. However, some Mordvins still strongly emphasize their ethnicity. This means that successful mission must be done in two languages, Moksha and Erzya. One of the biggest obstacles for successful mission is superstition.

Prayer Concerns:

1. Translate the Bible into both the Moksha and the Erzya languages.
2. Produce radio programs in both languages.
3. Plant churches among the Moksha and Erzya speaking people and pray for a revival with the Orthodox church.
4. Intensively proclaim the gospel. Awakening mission interest among the Mordvin believers for their own people.
5. Produce, print, and distribute good pamphlets and Christian literature among the Mordvins.

Mordvin

7.2 The Estonians

Population: 1,020,000
Language group: Finno-Ugrian language
Language: Estonian
Region: Estonia ASSR, Baltic Republics, and West Siberia
Capital: Tallinn (Reval)
Religion: Christian, including: Lutheran, Russian Orthodox, Methodists, Baptists, and Pentecostals.
Evangelicals: 80 to 100 thousand
Bible translation: available

Information:

In 1940, the Soviets occupied the small country of Estonia and officially added it as a state in the Soviet Union. However, opposition to the annexation still continues. People from other nations, especially Russians, are treated as foreigners in Estonia. Opposition to Russian occupation has helped the Estonians gain another status by the Russian government. We see this in church politics; for example, the Estonian churches have more freedom than any of the other Soviet churches.

In recent years, the Lutheran churches have started a revival and the Methodist and Baptist churches are carrying out vital mission work. Since 1986, the Baptists have printed a theological newspaper with an emphasis on young people. Many intellectuals, disappointed by the Marxist ideology, have been converted.

Prayer Concerns:

1. Continued revival in Estonia.
2. Plant new churches, especially in the northern and eastern regions of Estonia. Only a few Christians live in these areas.
3. Produce and distribute evangelistic literature.
4. Start television programs for Estonians, perhaps broadcast from Finland.
5. Awaken mission among the Estonian Christians for the Finno-Ugrian peoples in the Soviet Union.

7.3 The Udmurt

Population: 714,000
Language group: Finno-Ugrian language
Language: Udmurt
Region: Udmurt ASSR, on the western side of the Ural Mountains, between the Kama and Wjatka Rivers.
Capital: Ischewsk
Religion: Russian Orthodox
Evangelicals: Hundreds
Bible translation: the Four Gospels (1973)

Information:

The Udmurts have had a turbulent past. The Mongols reigned over the Udmurts until 1558. Since then, the Udmurts have belonged to the Russian kingdom. The Russian Orthodox Church missionized the Udmurts but without giving them a real sense of the Christian life. Even until today, many Udmurts, especially those in the prairie region, live as pagans. The urban population is atheistic. Only a few Udmurts have found the Savior Jesus Christ. Those who have are members of Russian speaking churches.

Prayer Concerns:

1. Translate the New Testament into Udmurt.
2. Start Udmurt speaking churches.
3. Convert Orthodox priests.
4. Awaken mission awareness among the Russian speaking churches in the Udmurt ASSR.
5. Send Christian missionaries to the Udmurt.

7.4 The Mari (Cheremiss)

Population: 622,000
Language group: Finno-Ugrian language
Language: Mari
Region: Mari ASSR, close to the Volga River
Capital: Joschkar-Ola
Religion: Christian/Russian Orthodox with strong pagan influence
Evangelicals: a few hundred
Bible translation: the New Testament (1985)

Information:

The Mari, earlier called the "Cheremiss," have three different ethnic backgrounds which are reflected in their dialects. Two of these dialects are very distinct: Lowland Mari and Highland Mari.

The Mari primarily work on collective farms. The Soviets have attempted to increase both the cultural and educational level of the Mari with only slight success.

The Orthodox Church has not had a major influence on the Mari people and Christianity has not been very influential. The atheistic propaganda has led to greater opposition to the Christian faith. Thus, only a few hundred Mari people are Christians today and they belong to Russian speaking churches.

Prayer Concerns:

1. Start Mari speaking churches.
2. Produce, print, and distribute evangelistic pamphlets, books, slides, and video-films in the Mari dialects.
3. Awaken mission awareness among the Mari Christians for doing mission among their own people.
4. Start Christian radio programs in Mari dialects.

7.5 The Komi (Zyryan)

Population: 327,000
Language group: Finno-Ugrian languages
Language: Komi
Region: Komi ASSR in the northeastern, European part of the USSR
Capital: Syktywkar (Komi ASSR)
Religion: Christians/Orthodox
Evangelicals: 0.5%
Bible translation: the New Testament (1980)

Information:

The Komi (Zyryan) are primarily fishermen and hunters, although some people prefer to live in cities. In the northern parts of the land, where Komi and Russians live together, people belong to a United Orthodox culture. Since the 14th and 15th centuries, the Komi have been Orthodox. However, the Christian faith does not appear to have any impact on their daily lives; rather, superstition and anxiety about spirits rule their lives.

In recent years, the young people have moved to the cities of the northern Ural Mountains where there is oil and gas production centers. These young people have a better education than their parents and, thus, they lose interest in tribal life. Some are discouraged by the atheistic teaching. At the beginning of this century, evangelical missionaries brought some Komi to a living faith in Christ. These people belong to Russian speaking churches.

Prayer Concerns:

1. Awaken mission interest among Christians in the USSR, especially those who live in Komi.
2. Plant churches in the cities and villages of Komi ASSR, especially in the capital Syktywkar.
3. The conversion of intellectuals among the Komi.
4. Translate the whole Bible into the Komi language.

7.6 The Permiak (Permyak)

Population: 151,000
Language group: Finno-Ugrian languages
Language: Komi-Permiak
Region: Komi-Permiak Autonomous districts in the eastern European part of the USSR)
Religion: Christian/Orthodox
Evangelicals: 0.5 %
Bible translation: the Gospel of Matthew

Information:

Experts estimate that the Permiaks lived in this region before the Russians came to the area. They have almost no cultural differences with the Russians, although one can detect certain ethnic distinctions.

In the 14th and 15th centuries, the Russian Orthodox Church missionized the Permiaks. The first mission to the Permiaks by bishop Stephan brought good spiritual fruit. Today, most Permiaks belong to the Orthodox church. Only a small group is evangelical and belongs to free churches; for example, the Baptist churches.

Prayer Concerns:

1. Translate the whole Bible into the Permiak language. Produce and transport the translated Bible sections to the region of Komi.
2. Awakening mission awareness among the churches in order to do mission among the Permiaks.
3. Plant Permiak churches which use their own language in worship.
4. Start prayer cells in the East and West for mission among the Permiaks.

7.7 The Hungarians

Population: 171,000
Language group: Finno-Ugrian languages
Language: Hungarian
Region: West Ukraine (Karpathian)
Religion: Christians/Evangelical-Reformed
Evangelicals: about 2,000
Bible translation: available

Information:

After World War II, the Soviets annexed a portion of Czechoslovakia and a small portion of Hungarians became part of the USSR; before World War I, they annexed the Czechoslovak West Karpathian Region (see 1.5 The Czechs and the Slovaks). More than 171,000 Hungarian people continue to live here today. The people are confronted with a difficult political situation because of the government's policies of russification.

The situation of the evangelical Christians is difficult. They do not have enough Christian literature or worship material in their own language. And, they rarely have contact with Christians in Hungary. The evangelicals in Hungary are busy with their own churches and it seems that they do not have time for the evangelicals in the Soviet Union. Thus, some Hungarian churches in the West Ukraine tend to speak more Russian than Hungarian. Unfortunately, Russian speaking churches cannot reach their neighbors who are nationalistically minded Hungarians.

Prayer Concerns:

1. Spiritual strength for the Hungarian churches in West Ukraine.
2. Theological education for Hungarian preachers and pastors (in their mother tongue).
3. Printing and transporting evangelistic literature for the Soviet-Hungarian people.
4. Awakening mission interest among Christians in Hungary for their own people in the Soviet Union.

7.8. The Karyalan (Karelian)

Population: 138,000
Language group: Finno-Ugrian languages
Language: Karelian
Region: Karelian ASSR in the northwestern part of the Soviet Union
Capital: Petrosawodsk
Religion: Christianity/Russian Orthodox
Evangelicals: a few hundred
Bible translation: the Gospel of John (1921)

Information:

Since the 12th century, the Karelians have lived under Russian rulers. Despite massive russification, they have obstinately maintained their national identity. Since the 1917 revolution, their language has been promoted in a socialistic manner. Related to the Veps, the Karelians work as farmers and have many animals. In the cities, especially in the Capital, many of them work in the wood industry.

The Karelian have not sufficiently had the true Gospel preached to them. Christianized by the Russian-Orthodox Church, the Christian life has remained foreign to the Karelian. Only a few hundred have become Christians. In the Capital of Petrosawodsk, there are some evangelical churches but most of them missionize the Russian rather than the Karelian population.

Prayer Concerns:

1. Translate the New Testament into the Karelian language,
2. Awaken mission interest among Karelian Christians for their people.
3. Produce and distribute evangelistic literature in the Karelian language.
4. Plant churches for the Karelian people
5. Salvation of the Orthodox priests who work among the Karelian population.

7.9 The Finns

Population: 77,000 in the Soviet Union
Language group: Finno-Ugrian languages
Language: Finnish
Region: Karelian ASSR and close to Leningrad
Religion: Christians/Evangelical-Lutheran
Evangelicals: about 5,000
Bible translation: available

Information:

Almost all Finns of the Soviet Union have lived under Soviet occupation since 1939. They do not have their own national status and are not easily accepted as Finns. Because of the complicated political situation, many Finns are resigned and disappointed. At the same time, this situation opens the Finns to hear the liberating gospel. The Evangelical-Lutheran, Baptist, and Pentecostal churches are growing. Belief in God has given them strength and national hope. Thus, by faith, Christian Finns in the Soviet Union have a living link to their brothers and sisters in Finland.

Prayer Concerns:

1. Growth of Finnish churches.
2. Theological education for pastors and church leaders of the Finnish speaking churches.
3. Transport evangelistic literature to the Soviet Finns.

7.10 The Khant (Ostyak) and the Vogul (Mansi)

The Khants

Population: 21,000
Language group: Finno-Ugrian languages
Language: Ostyak
Region: the Autonomous Region of Khant and Mansi, east of the Ural Mountains near the Ob River and its tributaries
Capital: Khanty-Mansi
Religion: animism
Evangelicals: none
Bible translation: the Gospel of Matthew (1868)

The Voguls

Population: 7,600
Language Group: Finno-Ugrian languages
Language: Mansi (Ob-Ugrian)
Region: the Autonomous Region of Khant and Mansi
Capital: Khanty-Mansi
Religion: animism
Evangelicals: none
Bible translation: Gospels of Matthew and Mark (1882)

Information:

The Khants and Voguls live in small groups scattered around the broad, western Siberian lowland. They came from the steppes of Eastern Russia to western Siberia during the first century A.D. Until 1581, the Tartars ruled over the Khants and Voguls. Thus, they adopted many of their cultural aspects from the Tatar people. In the 17th century, the Russians began occupying Siberia. People from both the Khants and the Voguls have been thrown into different regions and exploited by business people. With the addition of alcohol abuse and illness, many of them have become demoralized.

The life of the Khants and the Voguls includes three important aspects: hunting, fishing, and animal breeding. They collect nuts and berries and, for a beverage, they use birch juice.

All Khants and Voguls belong to either the group the *Mosch* or the group of the *Por*. It is prohibited to marry someone from the same group. They believe that the *Mosch* genealogy goes back to the rabbit and goose, while the *Por's* goes beck to the bear. In the winter and fall, both groups celebrate in their villages and make appropriate sacrifices. The Khants and the Voguls have many gods and believe in many spirits. Shamen mediate between the people and their gods. According to their beliefs, every man has five souls and every woman has four; animals have less, except bears who have the same number of souls as people do. The Khants and Voguls also believe in reincarnation.

Despite intensive collectivization and school programs, people from both nations retain their culture and religion. At the beginning of the 20th century, missionaries went to the Khants. The people repented at that time; however, today there are no Christians among either group.

Prayer Concerns:

1. Awaken mission awareness among the evangelical churches in west Siberia and Ural Mountains for the Khants and Voguls.
2. Print, transport, and deliver the translated gospels.
3. Translate the whole New Testament into the languages of the Khants and Voguls.
4. Send Christian missionaries to these people.
5. The salvation of school children and students from both nations in the cities of the Ural region.

7.11 The Lapps (Saami)

Population: 2,000
Language group: Finno-Ugrian languages
Language: Saamian; a written language of Saami was developed in the 1930s but was superseded by Russian
Region: Kola Peninsula
Religion: Christians/Russian Orthodox; animism
Evangelicals: unknown
Bible translation: available

Information:

Of 30,000 Lapps, only 2,000 live in the northwest region of the Soviet Union (the Kola Peninsula). They are hunters and animal breeders. The Skolt-Lapps, so-called in the Soviet Union, belong to the Russian Orthodox Church. Their brothers and sisters in Finland, Norway, and Sweden are Lutherans. Many of the Scandinavian Lapps live a Christ-dedicated life. They could play an important role in the mission enterprise of the Skolt-Lapps.

Prayer Concerns:

1. An adequate Bible translation into the Saamian language.
2. The conversion of intellectuals among the Lapps.
3. Church planting.
4. A turning away from animism.
5. The sending of missionaries to the Skolt-Lapps.
6. Radio programs from the Scandinavian Islands for the Lapps on the Kola Peninsula.

7.12 The Izhora

Population: a few hundred
Language group: Finno-Ugrian languages
Language: Izhora
Region: close to Leningrad
Religion: Christians/Russian Orthodox
Evangelicals: unknown
Bible translation: none

Information:

A small number of the Izhora people live in the region of Lononabow and Kingisepp, close to Leningrad. "The Land of the Izhora," as it is called, has belonged to Russia since 1702-1703. As result of this occupation, the Izhoras were scattered and robbed of almost all their rights. In spite of that, they remain a cohesive ethnic group which retains its own distinct language. However, they have many physical similarities with the Russian population. Most of the Izhoras work on farming.

Prayer Concerns:

1. A renewal among the Orthodox Izhoras and conversion of their priests.
2. The start of home Bible study groups with the emphasis on evangelism among the Izhoras.
3. An awakening of mission conscience among the Russian evangelicals for the Izhoras.

7.13 The Veps

Population: 8,100
Language group: Finno-Ugrian languages
Language: Veps/Russian
Region: Karelian ASSR, a region of Leningrad and Vologda
Religion: Christians/Orthodox
Evangelicals: unknown
Bible translation: none

Information:

The Veps, or "Lyudinikad," as they call themselves, are descendants of an old Baltic-Finnish people, the Vepsya. They live in small groups among with the Russian population. They primarily work in agriculture. All Veps speak the Russian language as well as their mother tongue. As a result of their shift to the Orthodox Church, they have tended to adapt to the Russian culture. It is possible that a few Veps are evangelical Christians.

Prayer Concerns:

1. Awakening mission interest among the evangelicals who live inthe region of the Veps.
2. Start prayer groups among the Karelians and Finns, who will pray for conversion of their "relatives".
3. The conversion of Vep Orthodox priests.
4. Start home churches with the purpose of reaching the Veps.

8. The Mongolian People

The four different Mongolian people groups in the Soviet Union have about 550,000 members and thus are one of the smallest people families. Originally from Central Asia, today they are scattered throughout the Soviet Union. The Buryats and Khalkha-Mongolians live in southeastern Siberia; the Kalmyks live east of southern Europe; and the Sart-Kalmyks live in Kirgizia and Uzbekhstan (Central Asia).

In addition to the common language and origin, their Buddhist religion binds them together. Monks from Tibet brought Lamaistic Buddhism to the people of Mongolia. Because the monks were well educated, they created a written language and organized schools for the Buryats and the Kalmyks. The Soviet government has tried to build a uniform culture and thus some of the Mongolian culture has been destroyed.

The Sart-Kalmyks, unlike the Buryats and Kalmyks, adapted to the Kirgizian culture and their religion — Islam.

The Russian Orthodox missionaries once worked among the Buryats before Buddhist missionaries came and seized the Buryats allegiance. It is not known if Christian believers are among the Buryats. Missions among the Kalmyks has been difficult, but the New Testament has been translated into their language. Unfortunately, this New Testament translation cannot be used today because the translators used the Tibetan alphabet. A new translation does not exist. No one has yet evangelized either the Khalkha-Mongolians or the Sart-Kalmyks.

Mission Concerns:

The peoples of Mongolia have not been reached with the gospel. The fact that they do not have churches means that they are dependent on the missionary activity of evangelical churches form other language groups. Evangelism among the people of Mongolia must become the responsibility of all Christians in the Soviet Union. The small Russian speaking churches in Kalmykia and Buryatia are unable to reach these people with the gospel. Christian churches are not known in the region of Khalkha-Mongolian. However, in Kirgizia, there are many German and Russian speaking churches with Baptists, Mennonites, Pentecostals, and Lutherans. These churches could easily reach the Sart-Kalmyks with the Gospel of Jesus Christ. Unfortunately, these churches lack experience and do not have a vision for this kind of work among other speaking peoples.

The churches in the West should try to motivate the Christians in the East. It is possible to translate the Bible in the West and send it to these groups. In addition, we can produce and send material for evangelism, video cassettes, and pamphlets to these people. A working relationship between the churches in East and West will soon bear fruit.

8.1 The Buryats

Population: 353,000
Language group: Mongolian languages
Language: Buryat
Region: Buryat ASSR (Baikal Sea in southern Siberia)
Capital: Ulan-Ude
Religion: Buddhism in the east; animism in the west
Evangelicals: none
Bible translation: the Gospels of Matthew and Mark (1975)

Information:

The Buryats live in the northern region of the ASSR. For hundreds of years they have been cattle farmers. They especially honor the horse.

The East and the West Buryats should be distinguished. The West Buryats had early contact with the Russian population and learned farming from them. The eastern region of the ASSR, where there is very dry land, the East Buryats have remained cattle herders.

In their beliefs they also have differences.

The beliefs of the East and West Buryats differ as well. The Eastern Buryats who live near the Baikal sea are Lamaistic Buddhists; the Western Buryats are Shamanists. Despite all the missionary outreach efforts by the Russian Orthodox church, the Buryats did not convert.

Prayer Concerns:

1. Awaken missionary interest among the evangelical churches in Siberia for the people of Buryat.
2. Print and distribute the New Testament.
3. Translate the Holy Scriptures into the Buryat language.
4. Send Christian missionaries to the Buryats.
5. The conversion of intellectuals in the capital Ulan-Ude.

Buryat

8.2 The Kalmyk (Kalmuk)

Population: 147,000
Language group: Mongolian languages
Language: Kalmyk
Region: Kalmyk ASSR, south of the Volga River
Capital: Elista
Religion: Buddhism
Evangelicals: none
Bible translation: the Four Gospels (1896)

Information:

The Kalmyks designate themselves, "Khal'mg". Originally, they lived in Central Mongolia. Until 1930, most of the Kalmyks were nomads. The life of the Kalmyks in the rural areas reveals signs of an earlier nomadic existence in spite of the Soviet government's attempt to change them.

In the capital Elista, a university with 4,400 students may be found. Buddhism is still deeply rooted in the minds of the Kalmyks. In the last decades, only a few people have accepted the Christian faith. It is unknown if any Kalmyks converted to Christianity.

Prayer Concerns:

1. Translate the Holy Scripture into the language of Kalmyks.
2. Awaken mission interest among the German and Russian Evangelical Christian-Baptists of Kalmykia.
3. Conversion of intellectuals in the capital Elista.

8.3 The Sart-Kalmyk

Population: a few thousand
Language group: Mongolian languages
Language: Sart-Kalmyk/Kirgiz
Region: the region of the Issyk-Kul Sea, Kirgizia SSR
Religion: Islam/Sunnite
Evangelicals: unknown
Bible translation: none

Information:

The Sart-Kalmyks belong to the west Mongolia branches of Olete. They came from China to Central Asia during the Dungan revolution of 1862-1877. Since 1884, they have lived in the same region where they live today.

More than other people groups, the Sart-Kalmyks have adapted to the Kirgizian culture. Most of them speak Kirgiz as their mother tongue. This adaptation is surprising because most of the Sart-Kalmyks live in more isolated, rural areas.

Prayer Concerns:

1. Awaken mission interest among the evangelical churches in the region for the Sart-Kalmyks.
2. Translate the New Testament into the Kirgiz language and transport these New Testaments into the Soviet Union.
3. Blessings for radio programs (TWR) in Kirgiz. Pray for programs in Sart-Kalmyk language.
4. The grounding of Bible study groups among Sart-Kalmyks.

8.4 The Khalkha-Mongolians

Population: 3,200
Language group: Mongolian languages
Language: Mongol
Region: southeastern Siberia
Religion: Buddhism
Evangelicals: unknown
Bible translation: none

Information:

The Khalkha-Mongols call themselves, "Khalkha," which means "shield". This region of northern Mongolia has been called "the shield" from the 16th century until now.

In the Soviet Union, the Khalkha live along the Mongolia/Soviet border. They are semi-nomadic cattle ranchers. They have almost no contact with people outside of their region.

The Khalkha have a Lamaistic Buddhist religious background that has become mixed with Shamanistic elements. No one knows if the Christian faith has reached the Khalkha.

Prayer Concerns:

1. Awaken missionary interest among the evangelical churches in the Soviet Union for the Mongolian peoples of Siberia.
2. Translate the Holy Scripture into the Khalkha language.
3. Send Christian "tentmakers" into this region.
4. Conversion of Mongolian students in the Soviet universities.

9. The Siberian People

Siberia is a large region; the seemingly endless taiga and tundra cover over ten million square km. In the past, many nomadic people groups inhabited Siberia; today nomads represent only 3% of the Siberian population. Approximately one million are original inhabitants.

The nomadic lifestyle remains an integral part of the Siberian peoples's lives, although the influence of the socialistic collectivization process is evident. Today, most Siberian people are part of collective farms which specialize in cattle breeding, agriculture, or hunting.

Modernity has slowly influenced the traditions of the Siberian people. The development of modernity has been accompanied by godlessness and societal illness. Many inhabitants are disoriented. Their traditional world-view — influenced by natural religions and Shamanism — is no longer sufficient; yet, the materialistic world-view of the Communists is foreign to them.

Only six of the 26 Siberian people groups have portions of the Bible translated into their language. Two of those have four gospels; two others have two gospels; the remaining two have only one Gospel available. Another problem is that many of these groups live in isolation and do not understand the Russian language. This presents difficulties in Bible translation. The Soviet linguists have done and continue to do important language studies that will make the missionary work easier in the future.

Mission Concerns:

The people of Siberia are open to the Gospel as never before. It is sad that there are no Christian churches in some of the regions where they live. Missionaries who would be willing to live and work in the difficult climatic conditions are needed. Such people could be engineers who work there in Soviet industry.

Christians who decide to move to this area must be educated. All missionary efforts must be accompanied by a thorough analysis of the religious and social world of these people. They have resisted the mission efforts of the Russian Orthodox church and the influences of atheism. In all major cities of South Siberia, there are evangelical churches. They are growing, but they tend to be limited to their own people groups. Only these Christians will be able to reach the Siberian people with the Gospel of Jesus Christ.

9.1 The Evenks (Tungus)

Population: 28,000
Language group: Tungus language
Language: Evenk
Region: Autonomous Area of the Evenks, Central Siberia; they are also found throughout Siberia from Yenisey River in the West to the Pacific Coast and Sakhalin Island in the East and to the Baikal Sea in the South. Some live in Mongolia and China.
Capital: Ture
Religion: animistic Shamanism
Evangelicals: unknown
Bible translation: not available

Information:

The Evenks, or Tungus, have a rich culture. Before the revolution in 1917, they were known as intelligent, honest, and hard working people. Under the pressure of the Yakuts and the Russians they dispersed throughout Siberia and north Manchuria. Under pressure from the Soviets, the Evenks social and cultural sentiments diluted. Until 1950, they resisted Soviet influence and collectivization.

The Evenks's written language was developed during the Soviet period. Today, almost all Evenks can read and write. The traditional culture is evident in their religious beliefs, despite strong persecution. For example, the Evenks believe that both good and evil spirits live in such things as trees and rocks. Although many Shamans have been killed in the past, Shamanism still exists. In the 17th and 18th centuries, the Russian Orthodox Church tried to Christianize the Evenks. In 1862, there were 9480 Christian Evenks registered. However, one wonders whether they truly became Christians because today there are no Christian churches among the Evenks.

Prayer Requests:

1. Awaken a missions interest among the Siberian churches for the Evenk people.
2. Translate the Bible for the Evenk people.
3. Send Christian missionaries to the Evenks.
4. Translate, produce, and transport evangelistic literature for the Evenks.

Ethnic Overview (excerpt) of Chapter 9

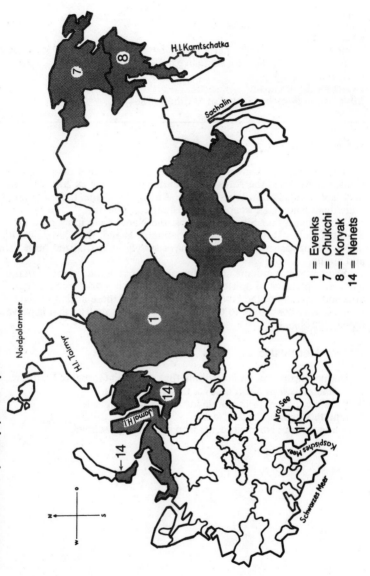

1 = Evenks
7 = Chukchi
8 = Koryak
14 = Nenets

H.I. Kamtschatka
Sachalin
Nordpolarmeer
H.I. Taimyr
Jamal H.I.
Aral See
Kaspisches Meer
Schwarzes Meer

9.2 The Nanai

Population: 10,500
Language group: Tungus language
Language: Nanai
Region: the eastern-most parts of the Soviet Union (on the lower Amur River and Sakhalin Island); some live in China.
Religion: animism
Evangelicals: unknown
Bible translation: the Gospel of Matthew (1884)

Information:

The Nanai, also known as the Golds, are an ancient people group. In Chinese chronicles the Nanai are mentioned as early as 2000 BC. Today, they have a highly developed culture. Among the Nanai there are talented individuals who make weapons and fishing equipment.

More than other Siberian groups, the Nanai have integrated into the Soviet society. Along the coast of Sakhalin Island, they have developed many fish processing plants; they have simply industrialized both fishing and hunting.

Shamanistic elements still influence their religion. Many Nanai have icons and pictures of spirits. Belief in the spirit world spreads fear. The atheistic teaching of the Soviets has not changed these ancient beliefs. This fear seems to contribute to the depression and alcoholism that is prevalent among the Nanai.

Prayer Requests:

1. Produce, transport, and distribute the translated Gospel of Matthew.
2. Awaken missions awareness for the Nanai people.
3. Translate the rest of the Bible into the Nanai language.
4. Send missionaries to the Nanai.
5. Evangelize the Nanai students who are in Soviet schools.

9.3 The Ulchi

Population: 1,900
Language group: Tungus language
Language: Ulchic
Region: Ulchic area in the Ansberovsk county in southeastern Siberia.
Religion: animism
Evangelicals: unknown
Bible translation: not available

Information:

The Ulchi inhabit areas along the lower Amur River. They call themselves Nanai. Over the centuries, their main occupation was fishing; hunting had only a secondary role. Today, they also work in agriculture even though the Amur River continues to be the life-stream of the Ulchi. To this day, the women continue to make clothes from fish skins.

Belief in spirits dominates the religion of the Ulchi. They make sacrifices to the spirits to ensure successful fishing.

There have been major changes for the Ulchi people in the 70 years of Soviet rule. These hunters and fishers have become farmers; hunting and fishing has become secondary.

Prayer Requests:

1. Awaken a mission interest among the evangelical churches in the Ansbarovsk region.
2. Send missionaries to the Ulchi.
3. Conversion of young Ulchi who study at the university in Ansbarovsk.

9.4 The Udegei

Population: 1,600
Language group: Tungus language
Language: Udegei
Region: the far eastern part of the Soviet Union between the Amur River and the Japanese Sea.
Religion: animistic Shamanism
Evangelicals: unknown
Bible translation: not available

Information:

The Udegei are good story tellers and have a rich tradition of fairy tales and legends that reflect their faith. They worship and make sacrifices to the spirits of forests, swamps, and other natural phenomena. The Udegei have a strong fear of death.

Under pressure from the Soviet government and through the process of education, the influence of traditional religion has weakened. Although Soviet linguists have developed a written language for the Udegei, the Russian language is increasingly more influential among them.

The Udegei have not been evangelized in the past.

Prayer Requests:

1. Awaken a mission interest for the Udegei among churches in the Komsoudsk region.
2. Send missionaries to the Udegei.
3. Develop, print, and transport good evangelistic literature for the Udegei.

9.5 The Orochi

Population: 1,200
Language group: Tungus language
Language: Orochic
Region: the far eastern parts of the Soviet Union
Religion: 98% animists; about 1% Buddhists; about 1% Christian.
Evangelicals: unknown
Bible translation: not available

Information:

Most Orochi live in villages in the far eastern parts of the Soviet Union. In the past, they were hunters and fishermen. Today, they are cattle, sheep, and horse breeders. Many Orochi are talented blacksmiths. They also grow some wheat and soy.

Belief in the spirit world influences the religion of the Orochi. They believe that everything has a spirit. The Shamans make sacrifices — pigs, chickens, or dogs — in special buildings so that the spirits will protect them and bring success in their work. During funerals they have similar sacrificial ceremonies. Only a few Orochi have been converted to Buddhism or to Christianity.

Prayer Requests:

1. Conversion of the nominal Christians among the Orochi.
2. Awaken missions interest among far eastern Christians for the Orochi.
3. Awaken a mission interest among Orochi Christians, if there are any, for their own people.
4. Develop good evangelistic literature for the Orochi people.

9.6 The Negidal

Population: 500
Language group: Tungus language
Language: Negidalic
Region: the far eastern parts of the Soviet Union on the lower Amgun and Amur Rivers.
Religion: ancestor worship; animism
Evangelicals: unknown
Bible translation: not available

Information:

The Negidal people are hunters and fishermen. Although today they live on collective farms, their lifestyle has changed little. They still have tribal organization, each tribe worshipping their own ancestors and spirits. Special tribal prayers are given before the hunting season and all the Negidal celebrate a "Feast of the Bear."

On the collective farms, Negidal work together with Russians. Through that interactive process with the Russians, many Negidal have adapted to the russification policies of the Soviet Union. This russification, or integration, may be why the Negidal people have not been listed in the Population Statistic since 1929. However, the fact that they are being listed once again in the new statistics reflects the growing national awareness of this small people group.

Prayer Requests:

1. Awaken a mission interest among far eastern evangelical churches for the Negidal people.
2. Send missionaries to the Negidal people.
3. Distribute portions of the Bible among the Negidal.
4. Show Christian video films among the Negidal.
5. Conversion of Negidal and church planting.

9.7 The Chukchi

Population: 14,000
Language group: Paleoasiatic
Language: chukchi
Region: Autonomous Region in the upper northeastern Soviet Union
Religion: Shamanism
Evangelicals: unknown
Bible translation: not available

Information:

The Chukchi are divided into two groups: the Racing Chukchi, also called the "Chavchuven," and the Coastal Chukchi, who call themselves, "An'Kalyn". Their lifestyle is similar to Greenland's Eskimos. As with the many other Siberian people groups, the worship of spirits plays an important role in the day to day life of the Chukchi. Fear of spirits and Shamanistic practices dominate the lives of many. Depression and other emotional problems are widespread. The atheistic "liberation" has not changed this condition.

There is no Christian witness among the Chukchi.

Prayer Requests:

1. Awaken a mission interest among evangelical churches in the USSR and Alaska for the Chukchi people.
2. Send radio broadcasts in the Chukchi language from Alaska.
3. Send Christian missionaries to the Chukchi people.

Evenk

Chukchi

Nenet

9.8 The Koryak

Population: 7,900
Language Group: Paleosastic
Language: Koryak
Region: Autonomous Region of Koryak on the Kamchatka Peninsula.
Religion: animism with ancestor worship
Evangelicals: unknown
Bible translation: not available

Information:

The Koryak live in the northern part of the Kamtshata Peninsula. Those living along the coast are fishers and hunters and those living inland are cattle breeders. The lifestyles of the coastal Koryaks and the cattle-breeding Koryaks differs significantly; nevertheless, they maintain a common culture and common religious expressions. Their cultures exhibit diversification, similar to other Siberian groups, and their religious rituals serve to soften the spirits. But, Shamans play a rather insignificant role.

Today, the Koryaks are collectivized. Children study in interment schools. The Soviets have done a great deal to educate a strong group of intellectual Koryaks who can carry on their cultural traditions. As a result, there are Koryak teachers, doctors, and writers. Attempts by the Russian Orthodox Church to evangelize the Koryaks have not been successful. The Koryaks are still waiting for the saving gospel of Jesus Christ.

Prayer Requests:

1. Awaken mission interest among Christian professionals who find work in Kamchatka.
2. Develop Christian literature for the Koryaks.
3. Conversion of Koryak intellectuals.
4. Send missionaries to the Koryaks.

9.9 The Itelmen

Population: 1,400
Language group: Paleoasastic
Language: Itemenic
Region: the west coast of the Kamchatka Peninsula
Religion: Shamanism
Evangelicals: none
Bible translation: not available

Information:

The Itelmen are the original inhabitants of the Kamchatka Peninsula. In the past, they were called "Kamchadal". Their lifestyle and culture were highly developed and the first Russian settlers intermarried with them and became Itelmen.

These first Russian settlers brought a Christian influence to the Itelmen. Strange forms of Christianity are still evident, although Shamanism and animism prevail. The continually decreasing numbers of Itelmen may be explained by the process of russification.

Prayer Requests:

1. Awaken a mission interest among the evangelical churches for the Itelmen.
2. Conversion of Orthodox priests who work among the Itelmen.
3. Conversion of the nominal Christians among the Itelmen.
4. Print and distribute evangelistic literature.

9.10 The Eskimos

Population: 1,500
Language group: Paleoasatic
Language: Eskimo
Region: Chukchi Peninsula and Vrangel Island (west of Alaska)
Religion: Shamanism
Evangelicals: unknown
Bible translation: available

Information:

The Eskimo people mainly live in North America and Greenland. Approximately 1,500 live in the USSR and are thoroughly integrated with the Chukchi.

Animism and Shamanism influence their religion. Some say they have contacts with North American Eskimos. Christians are unknown among them.

Prayer Requests:

1. Awaken mission interest among Soviet churches and North American Eskimo churches for their brothers and sisters in the USSR.
2. Start radio broadcasts from Alaska in the Eskimo language.
3. Send Christian missionaries to the Eskimo people.
4. Transport and distribute the Eskimo Bible.

9.11 The Gilyak (Nivkhi)

Population: 4,400
Language group: Paelasatic
Language: Nivkhi
Region: the far eastern regions of the Soviet Union, from the lower Amur River to Sakhalin Island
Religion: nominal Christianity with animistic influences
Evangelicals: unknown
Bible translation: not available

Information:

The Nivkhi, in the past called the "Gilyaks," belong to the old Siberian people group. They are fishermen and hunters. Only a few have found their way to cities. But, even in cities they stay close together. The language of the Nivkhi is dying. Less than 50% speak Nivkhi, while the others speak Russian (although the Russians have difficulty understanding it).

Before the Revolution of 1917, the Nivkhi belonged to the Russian Orthodox Church, but Christianity never developed. An animistic belief in spirits dominates their religious life until today. The Nivkhi still await for the day when they will be freed through the power of Christ's Gospel.

Prayer Requests:

1. Awaken mission interest among the evangelical churches for the Nivkhi people.
2. Conversion of Orthodox priests who work with the Nivkhi.
3. Conversion of Nivkhi who live in cities.
4. Send Christian missionaries to the Nivkhi region.

9.12 The Ket

Population: 1,200
Language group: Paleoasatic
Language: Ketic
Region: Siberia; Central region around the Yenisey River
Religion: animism
Evangelicals: unknown
Bible translation: not available

Information:

The Kets have lived for more than a millennium in Siberia. Previously nomadic people, today they have been collectivized and work at farming furs and breeding for racing.

The Kets are animists. They believe that a person has seven souls which travel between members of a tribe. After one is dead, these souls are reborn in their children. Their relationship to the spirits, both good and evil, are channeled by Shamans.

Today, most Kets can read and write. Their language is also taught in schools. Their religious world is still the same as in the past. The Kets live without a single Christian witness.

Prayer Requests:

1. Awaken a mission interest among evangelical churches in Siberia for the Kets.
2. Send missionaries into the Ket region.
3. Send Christian teachers to the secular preschools where Ket children study.
4. Conversion of Ket intellectuals.

9.13 The Yukagir

Population: 600
Language group: Paleoasatic
Language: Yukagiric
Region: northeastern Yakut ASSR, along the upper Kolyma River and in the Tundra between the Indigirka and Alasia Rivers
Religion: animism
Evangelicals: unknown
Bible translation: not available

Information:

The Yukagir are a nomadic people and work in reindeer breeding. During the winter, they are less nomadic and live in wooden houses on collective farms.

Shamans continue to have a very significant role in the Yukagirs' lives. They are worshiped after their death and sacrifices are made to them.

Increasingly, more children and youth leave the region to study in schools. For them, the traditional beliefs lose meaning. Consequently, there is an opportunity for the gospel.

Prayer Requests:

1. Evangelization of the Yukagir youth and children who often study in schools several hundred kilometers away from home.
2. Distribute Christian literature among the Yukagir.
3. Send missionaries to the Yukagir.

9.14 The Nenets

Population: 30,000
Language Group: Samoyedic
Language: Nenetic
Region: Autonomous Region of the Nenets, Dolgan, and Yamal-Nenets (northwestern Siberia)
Religion: nominal Christianity with strong animistic influences
Evangelicals: a few
Bible translation: not available

Information:

The Nenets are the largest group of the Nordic Peoples and inhabit a large territory. They are reindeer breeders. Despite many State attempts to integrate them, the Nenets maintain their original lifestyle. They live under difficult climatic conditions. There is usually snow for 260 days of the year and the temperatures drop below 50 degrees centigrade.

Until the 19th century, the Nenets were strongly influenced by animism. In the 19th century, the Russian Orthodox missionaries were successful in converting the majority of them and, by the end of the century, all the Nenets were baptized. However, they continued many of their pagan rituals. They now included St. Nicholas into their religion, even bringing sacrifices to him and putting animal blood and pelt on icons. The Shamans did not disappear. Through today, there are strong Shamanistic expressions.

Prayer Requests:

1. Awaken a mission interest among evangelical churches for the Nenets.
2. Start mission outreach.
3. Translate the Bible into the Nenets language.
4. Conversion of Orthodox priests who serve among the Nenets.
5. Find and equip the nominal Christians.

9.15 The Nganasan (Tavgi Sameyed)

Population: 900
Language group: Samoyedic
Language: Nganasan
Region: Tayamyr Peninsula in northern Siberia (Dolgen and Nenets Autonomous Region)
Religion: Shamanism
Evangelicals: unknown
Bible translation: not available

Information:

The Nganasans (in the past known as the "Tavgi Samoyed") call themselves "Nya," which means "comrade". They are involved in reindeer breeding. Although they live with other people groups on collective farms, today they maintain their national independence. Approximately 200 Nganasans live outside the Tayamyr Peninsula.

The Nganasans are Shamanists, although they have developed a unique understanding about the unity between the material and the spiritual. Access to the spirits and appeasing those spirits is only for the Shamans. More than neighboring people groups, the Nganasans continue to practice their religion and this concerns the Soviet authorities. The 900 Nganasans live without a Christian witness.

Prayer Requests:

1. Awaken a mission interest among the evangelical churches in the USSR for the Nganasans.
2. Send missionaries to the Nganasans.
3. Conversion of Nganasans who have left their traditional region and are disconnected from the traditions of their fathers.

9.16 The Selkup (Ostyak-Samoyed)

Population: 3,600
Language group: Samoyedic
Language: Selkup
Region: the Yamal-Nenets Autonomous Region between the Ob and Yenisey Rivers in northeastern Siberia
Religion: Shamanism
Evangelicals: unknown
Bible translation: not available

Information:

In the past, the Selkup were called "East-Samoyedi". They are reindeer breeders and today live on collective farms. Their settlements often directly neighbor other Siberian tribes and European settlers. Despite these close contacts they strongly maintain their national traditions and culture.

The Selkups's religion is similar to other Siberian people and many Selkups live in fear of spirits.

Prayer Requests:

1. Awaken mission interest among evangelical churches in the USSR for the Selkup.
2. Send missionaries to the Selkups.
3. Conversion of Selkup leaders.

9.17 The Aleuts

Population: 500
Language group: Eskimo-Aleutian
Language: Unangan
Region: Komandirovskiy Islands to the east of the Kamehatka Peninsula
Religion: Christianity/Orthodox
Evangelicals: unknown
Bible translation: not available

Information:

The Aleuts call themselves "Unangan." Their name describes that they originated from the Aleutian Islands. In the Soviet Union, the Aleuts live on the Komandir Islands where they moved in the 19th century. The majority of these people have occupations in the fishing industry.

Through a continuous assimilation with other groups, especially the Russians, the number of Aleuts is decreasing. The Soviets have shown little interest in developing the language and culture of the Aleuts.

The Aleuts were Christianized in the 19th century. With the missionaries came colonists who demoralized the Aleutian people and destroyed their culture. Because of such negative influence, the Aleutians's Christian faith never developed.

Prayer Requests:

1. Awaken a mission interest among the evangelical churches for the Aleut people.
2. Send "tentmaker" missionaries to the Aleuts.
3. Conversion of Orthodox priests who serve in this region.
4. Conversion of Aleutian leaders.

10. Other People Groups

All people groups, which do not live in a specific region in the Soviet Union or do not belong to any of the previously mentioned people groups, come under this heading. "Other people groups" include the Germans, Jews, Greeks, Gypsies, Koreans, Chinese, and others. Some of these groups are small, others have millions, such as the Jews and the Germans.

As people who have moved into the Soviet Union's geographical area, they have only limited political rights. Only the Jews have an autonomous region in the far east and, even then, only a few Jews inhabit this region.

Religiously, people from these groups belong to Islam (e.g., the Dungans), to Christianity (e.g., the Germans and the Greeks), or to Buddhism (e.g., the Koreans). Evangelical Christians are particularly found among the Germans. The Germans have the highest percentage of the evangelical Christians in the Soviet Union. Only a few evangelical Christians are found among the Greeks and Assyrians. There are only about ten Korean Christians; among the Dungans, there is no record of a single Christian.

Mission Concern:

The German evangelical churches are spread throughout the different regions of the Soviet Union. At the present, there is only a limited vision for missions within these churches. Their services are usually conducted in German, a language which the surrounding people do not understand. But, these churches are strategically very important. They need to be motivated, prepared, and then sent to the mission fields of unreached people.

Other immigrant people groups seem to be even less interested in mission. Although there is a revival in Korea, there is no significant manifestation of this revival among the 400,000 Koreans in the Soviet Union. This large group of Koreans in the USSR is simply neglected. In order to reach these people, we need to motivate the Korean Christians to do something for their brothers and sisters in the Soviet Union.

Similar things could be said about the Chinese Dungans. Because they live in closed communities, Chinese Christians from outside the Soviet Union might be the best people to missionized the Chinese in the USSR. Perhaps, after establishing good contact, the work could be continued by the other Soviet Christians. Similar things could be said about the Greeks.

The mission minded Christians in the Soviet Union urgently need prayer for, and practice in, doing mission to reach these "other people groups" for the LORD.

10.1 The Jews

Population: 1,811,000
Language group: Semitic language
Language: Yiddish, Evrit (only 1/7 of the Soviet Jews speak their language)
Region: throughout the European part of the USSR. Only a few (10,200) live in the Autonomous Jewish Region in the far east.
Capital: Birobidshan (Jewish Autonomous Region)
Religion: 10% Jewish, 80% Atheist, 5% Orthodox
Evangelicals: 0.5%
Bible translation: available

Information:

Jews have lived within the territory of today's Soviet Union for many centuries. Their history reflects suffering and persecution. Despite these facts, the Jews maintain strong cultural ties, probably because of their strong intellectual commitments. This cohesion is reflected in their urbanizing tendencies.

The majority of Soviet Jews are secularized. Only 10% still adhere to the beliefs of their fathers. In some areas, the Russian Orthodox and the evangelicals have had some missionary success. There is even a church known to have primarily Jewish believers.

The political situation is difficult for the Jews. Many seek to leave the country. Among the Jewish immigrants, especially in the USA, some mission work is done.

Prayer Concerns:

1. For the few Jewish believers and their testimony among their people.
2. Awaken mission interest in the evangelical churches in the Soviet Union for the Jews.
3. For testimonies from those who immigrated to the West and converted Jews who speak to their relatives in their old homeland.

10.2 The Central Asian Jews (Bukharan)

Population: several thousand
Language group: Iranian language
Language: Tadzhik
Region: large cities in Uzbek and Tadzhik SSR, like Samarkand, Tashkent, Bukhara, Kokand, Dushanbe
Religion: Judaism
Evangelicals: unknown
Bible translation: New Testament (1983)

Information:

There is little known about the origin of the Bukharan Jews. For centuries they have built their own social group in the Central Asian cities. Bukhara is one of their centers. Today, they speak a dialect of the Tadzhik language and have developed their own culture. Many Bukharan Jews are involved in the arts, sciences, and have significant cultural influence.

Little is known about the religious, organizational structure of the Bukharan Jews.

Prayer Requests:

1. Awaken a mission interest among Christian Jews in the Soviet Union for the Bukharan Jews.
2 Distribute the Tadzhik New Testament.
3. Start a house Bible group in Dushanbe where a lange number of the Bukharan Jews live.
4. Conversion of key persons who have influence in the community.

10.3 The Germans

Population: 1.936 million; 1.05 million in Central Asia
Language group: Germanic
Language: German and Russian (1.1 million view German as their mother tongue)
Region: more than half of the Germans live in Central Asia in Kazakhstan, Tadzhikistan, and Uzbekistan. Others live in the European North Ural region and Siberia. Small groups live in the Ukraine, Moldavia, and in the Baltic Republics
Religion: 65% Protestants, Lutherans and Reformed; 30% Catholics
Evangelicals: about 200,000
Bible translation: available

Information:

The Germans in the Soviet Union are descendants of the 18th and 19th century immigrants. Their motives to immigrate to Russia were often religious in nature; their cultural traditions and rituals have strong Christian aspects. The number of the evangelicals is high. In comparison to other people groups in the Soviet Union, the Germans have the highest percentage of born-again Christians. They presently have a strong influence on the evangelical churches in the USSR.

Politically, they have a small voice. Since the loss of their Autonomous Republic during World War II, they have had little chance to move forward. The loss explains the emigration wave of Germans to the West. In recent years, this group has developed an increasing interest in mission work among the unreached people in the Soviet Union.

Prayer Requests:

1. Increase mission interest among the German churches for their own people.
2. Wisdom to know the appropriate level of political involvement so as not to confuse their priorities.
3. Biblical, theological education for church leaders.
4. New possibilities to bring in Christian German literature for believers.

10.4 The Gypsies

Population: 209,000
Language group: Indo-Germanic
Language: Roman
Region: throughout the USSR; there is a large group in Moldavia and the western Ukraine
Religion: spiritism
Evangelicals: about 5%
Bible translation: the Gospel of John (1933 for Latvia)

Information:

The Soviet Gypsies belong to the Roman Gypsies. Known worldwide as a wandering people, they have migrated all over the Soviet Union. Attempts to help them settle did not have great results. The Christian mission of the Russian Orthodox Church has not gained access to the nature-loving Gypsies.

Only in recent years has there been an awakening among the Gypsies in Moldavia and in the Ural Mountains.

Today, there are several Gypsy churches with charismatic emphases. They are known for their strong mission efforts.

Prayer Requests:

1. Equip the Christian Soviet Gypsies.
2. Biblical, pastoral education in the Gypsy churches.
3. Openness in receiving newly converted Gypsies.
4. Conversion of Gypsy leaders.
5. Distribute Christian literature for the Roman speaking Gypsies.

10.5 The Koreans

Population: 390,000
Language Group: Mongolian
Language: Korean and Russian; about 55%, especially the older generations, can read and write their mother language.
Region: most Koreans live in the Soviet Republic of Kazakistan (Kzyl-Orda Region, east of the Aral Sea)
Religion: Buddhism and Confucianism; the younger generation is not religious
Evangelicals: a few
Bible translation: available

Information:

Koreans in the Soviet Union are known as good vegetable farmers and business people. Most Koreans are bilingual, speaking Korean and Russian, and they are culturally open. Contact with their homeland is very weak; the Buddhist and Confucian influence is also weak. The youth are not religious and are not particularly influenced by the atheistic propaganda either.

For several years there has been a small Korean church. In the past, some of the Korean Christians were imprisoned because of missionary activities.

Prayer Requests:

1. Spiritual awakening among Koreans in the USSR, such as the revival in Korea today.
2. Missionaries who would bring the gospel to Koreans in their language.
3. Possibilities to send Korean Bibles to the USSR and distribute them.
4. Spiritual church growth among the Christian home groups.
5. Radio broadcasting for the Soviet Koreans.

10.6 The Dungans

Population: 52,000
Language group: Mongolian
Language: Chinese
Region: In the region of Prashewalsk and Osh in the Kirgiz SSR and Uzbek SSR
Religion: Islam/Sunnite
Evangelicals: unknown
Bible translation: not available

Information:

Culturally, the Dungans belong to the Chinese. Their Chinese language is strongly influenced by Arabic, Persian, and Turkish. As a rule, many Dungans speak the Kirgiz language in addition to their own. Young people also speak Russian.

The Dungans came to Central Asia after a revolt in China known as the Dungan Revolt of 1862-1877. Today, the Dungans work primarily in agriculture, growing rice and vegetables. Some are involved in growing opium. Only a few Dungans live in cities.

Prayer Requests:

1. Translate portions of the Bible into the Dungan language.
2. Distribute available Russian and Kirgiz Christian literature among Dungans.
3. Awaken mission interest among evangelical churches in Kirgiz for the Dungans.
4. Conversion of influential Dungans and beginning of house churches.

10.7 The Assyrians (Nestorians)

Population: 25,000
Language group: Semitic
Language: Assyric
Region: Armenian SSR
Religion: Orthodox Christians
Evangelicals: unknown
Bible translation: available

Information:

The Aturai, as the Assyrians call themselves, are followers of the Christian Nestorian emigrants from Turkey and Iran. After suffering religious persecution in Turkey and Iran, at the turn of the century, they left and immigrated to what is now the USSR. Today, they live in Armenia SSR where they work in agriculture. Many have moved to cities along the Black Sea coast and work in industry or in service professions.

The Assyrians are nominal Christians and organized religious practice is not available. Young Assyrians can be described as completely secularized.

Prayer Requests:

1 Publish and distribute the Assyrian Bible.
2 Awaken mission interest among the Armenian Christians for the Assyrians.
3. Start Assyrian home study groups in the cities.
4. Conversion of nominal Assyrian believers and starting a church with a Biblical orientation.

10.8 Arabs

Population: unknown
Language group: Semitic
Region: central and southern area of the Seravshan River in the Uzbeck SSR and in southern Tadzhik SSR
Religion: Islam/Sunnite
Evangelicals: unknown
Bible translation: available

Information:

The Central Asian Arabs have lived for centuries in the region where they live today — southern Uzbeck SSR and southern Tadzhik SSR. Long ago, they adapted to the Uzbeck and Tadzhik cultures. Despite this enculturalization, a portion of the Arabs maintain their cultural distinctives. Their rural settlements are conducive to this type of independence. Because the Arabic language is not used in the USSR, the Arabs are left without a written language. But, because of a growing national or ethnic awareness, interest in their own language is growing.

Bibles in Arabic are not available in the Soviet Union. Bringing in Arabic Bibles might help awaken an interest in the Christian faith.

Prayer Requests:

1. Transport and distribute Arabic Bibles to the USSR.
2. Awaken a mission interest among Central Asian churches for the Arabs.
3 Send Christian-Arabic students from the third world to study in Central Asia with a goal of mission outreach.
4. Conversion of secularized Arabs in the cities.

10.9 The Greeks

Population: 344,000
Language group: Greek
Language: Greek and Turkish
Region: Georgian SSR; Krasnodar Region, northeast of the Black Sea coast
Religion: Christianity/Greek Orthodox
Evangelicals: unknown
Bible translation: available

Information:

There have been Greek settlements in the Black Sea area for centuries. At the beginning of this century, a large group of Greeks moved from Iran and Turkey to Caucasus. They lived in cities along the coast and they became involved in trading. One group of the Caucasian Greeks, the so-called "Urums," speak a dialect of the Turkish language; the Greek speaking Greeks in Caucasus are called the "Romeo".

A large Greek population is also in Central Asia. These Greeks are recent immigrates to the USSR. The Greek Orthodox Christians have no organized church life in the Soviet Union. Only a few have access to the Word of God in their own language.

Prayer Requests:

1. Transport Greek Bibles to the Soviet Christians.
2. Conversion of Orthodox priests and starting Biblical churches among the Greeks.
3. Awaken a mission interest among the Soviet churches for their Greek neighbors.
4. Start radio broadcasts in the Greek language.
5. Mission efforts among the Turkish speaking Urums.

APPENDIX

Table 1:

The ethnic composition of the Soviet population (1979)
(Only the larger groups)

People Group	Population (in 1000s)	% of whole population	national language as mother language (in %)	Russian as a 2nd language (in %)
Russians	137397	52.42		
Ukrainians	42347	16.16	82.8	49.8
Uzbeks	14456	4.75	98.5	49.3
Belorussians	9463	3.61	74.2	57.0
Kazakhs	6556	2.50	97.5	52.3
Tatars	6317	2.41	85.9	68.9
Azerbaidzhans	5400	2.09	97.9	29.5
Armenians	4151	1.58	90.7	38.6
Georgians	3433	1.36	98.3	26.7
Moldavians	2968	1.13	93.3	47.4
Tadzhiks	2898	1.10	97.8	29.6
Lithuanians	2851	1.09	97.9	52.1
Turmen	2028	·0.77	98.7	25.4
Germans	1936	0.74	57.0	51.7
Kirgiz	1906	0.73	97.9	29.4
Jews	1811	0.69	14.2	13.7
Chuvash	1751	0.67	81.7	64.8
People Groups of Dagestan	1657	0.63	95.9	60.3
Latvians	1439	0.55	95.0	56.7
Bashkirs	1371	0.52	67.0	64.9
Mordvins	1192	0.45	72.6	65.5
Polish People	1151	0.44	29.1	44.7
Estonians	1020	0.39	95.3	24.2
Chechen	756	0.28	78.97	61.55
Udmurts	714	0.27	76.5	64.4
Mari	622	0.24	86.7	69.9
Ossetian	542	0.21	88.2	64.9
Koreans	390	0.15	55.4	47.7
Bulgarians	365	0.14	68.0	58.2
Buryats	353	0.13	90.2	71.0
Greeks	344	0.13	38.0	34.1
Komi	327	0.13	76.2	64.5
Yakuts	328	0.12	95.3	55.6
Kabardins	322	0.12	97.7	77.1
Karakalpaks	303	0.12	95.9	45.1

Uigurs	211	0.08	86.1	52.1
Gypsies	209	0.08	74.1	59.1
Ingushs	186	0.071	97.0	
Gagauzs	173	0.066	89.0	
Hungarians	171	0.065		
Tuvins	166	0.063	98.8	59.2
People Groups of the North	158	0.06		
Permyaks	151	0.058	77.0	
Kalmyks	147	0.056	91.3	84.1
Karalians	138	0.053	55.6	51.3
Karachai	131	0.05	98.0	

Table 2:

People Groups, Languages, and Bible Translations

People Groups	Population	% of ethnic group that speaks mother language	Recent Bible Translation until 1985
Slavic peoples			
Russians	137,397,000	100	available
Ukrainians	42,347,000	83	available
Belorussians	9,463,000	74	available
Poles	1,151,000	29	available
Bulgarians	365,000	68	available
Czechs	18,000	?	available
Slovaks	9,400	?	available
Non-Slavic people groups			
Uzbeks	2,456,600 M	99	Genesis*, John* (1982), IBT
Kazaks	6,556,000 M	98	Luke* (1983), IBT
Tatars	6,317,000 M	86	4 Gospels* & Acts* (1985), IBT
Azerbaidzhans	5,477,000 M	98	NT* (1982), IBT, Children's Bible (1986)
Armenians	4,151,000	91	Bible (1978), IBT, Children's Bible (1986)
Georgians	3,571,000	98	NT* (1985), IBT
Moldavians	2,968,000	93	NT* (1983), Bible* (1984), IBT, First
Tadzhiks	2,898,000 M	98	NT* (1983), IBT, First NT
Lithuanians	2,851,000	98	
Turkmen	2,028,000 M	99	John* (1982), IBT
Germans	1,936,000	57	continuous
Kirgiz	1,906,000	98	Acts* 1984 IBT, Mk. u. Luke (1987)

* = New Translation
First = First Christian literature in this language
IBT = Published by Institute for Bible Translation
M = Muslims
B = Buddhists

People Groups	Population	% of ethnic group that speaks mother language	Recent Bible Translation until 1985
Chuvash	1,751,000	82	John *(1984), IBT
Latvians	1,439,000	95	
Bashkirs	1,371,000	67	4 Gospels (1975), IBT
Mordvins	1,192,000	73	4 Gospels (1973), IBT
Estonians	1,020,000	95	
Chechens	756,000 M	79	John * & Acts *, IBT, First
Udmurts	714,000	77	4 Gospels (1973), IBT
Mari	622,000	87	John * (1985), IBT
Ossetians	542,000 M	88	John * (1984), IBT
Avars	483,000 M	98	John * (1979), IBT First
Lezgins	383,000 M	91	not available
Buryats	353,000 B	90	Mt., Mk. (1975), IBT
Yakuts	328,000	95	4 Gospels (1975), IBT
Komi	327,000	76	NT* (1980), IBT, NT First
Kabadians	322,000 M	98	not available
Karakalpaks	303,000 M	96	not available
Dargins	287,000 M	98	not available
Kumyks	228,000 M	96	Mt., Mk. (1897)
Uigurs	211,000 M	86	Mk. (1982), IBT NT (Arab) repr. (1986)
Gypsies	209,000	74	John (1933) f. Zigeuner in Lettland
Ingushes	186,000 M	97	not available
Gagauzs	173,000	89	Mt.(1975), IBT
Tuvins	166,000 B	99	not available
Permiaks	151,000	77	Mt., IBT
Kalmyks	147,000 B	91	4 Gospels (1896)
Karelian	138,000	56	John (1921)
Karachai	131,000 M	98	Mk.* (1978), IBT, First
Adygei	109,000 M	96	Mk. (1977)
Abkhaz	91,000 M	94	John* (1981), IBT
Laks	86,000	95	not available

People Groups	Population	% of ethnic group that speaks mother language	Recent Bible Translation until 1985
Tabasarans	75,000 M	97	not available
Khakasses	71,000	81	not available
Balkers	66,000 M	97	not available
Altai	60,000	86	4 Gospels (1975), IBT
Nogai	60,000 M	90	4 Gospels (1925)
Dungans	52,000 M	95	not available
Khakess	46,000 M	91	not available
Nenets	30,000	80	not available
Abazas	29,000 M	95	not available
Evenks	28,000	43	not available
Tats	22,000	67	not available
Khants	21,000	68	Matt. (1868)
Shors	16,000	61	not available
Rutuls	15,000 M	99	not available
Zachurs	14,000 M	95	not available
Chukchi	14,000	78	not available
Nanai	10,500	56	Matt. (1884)
Aguls	10,000	98	not available
Koryaks	7,900	69	not available
Mansi	7,600	50	Mt., Mk. (1882)
Dolgans	5,100	90	4 Gospels (1975)
Nivkhi	4,400	31	not available
Slkups	3,600	57	not available

Other people groups and foreign minorities: 6,783,900 (incl. 1.8 million Jews)

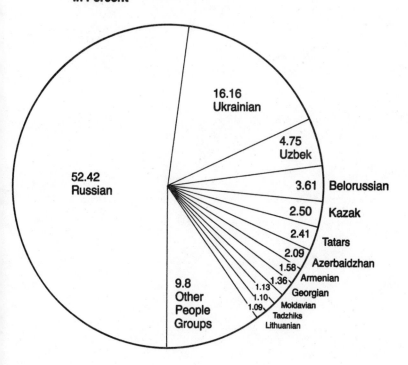

**Ethnic Composition
of the Soviet Population (1979)
in Percent**

52.42
Russian

16.16
Ukrainian

4.75
Uzbek

3.61 Belorussian

2.50 Kazak

2.41 Tatars

2.09 Azerbaidzhan

1.58 Armenian

1.36 Georgian

1.13 Moldavian

1.10 Tadzhiks

1.09 Lithuanian

9.8
Other
People
Groups

BIBLIOGRAPHY

Part 1:

Amburger, Erik, Geschichte des Protestantismus in Rubland, 1961.
Brandenburg, H, Christen im Schatten der Nacht,Wuppertal 1974.
Kahle, W., Evangelische Christen in Rubland und der Sowjetunion, Wuppertal und Kassel 1978.
Kelelnik, S.B., Sovyetski Soyuz. Obschi Obzor, Moskau 1972.
Gurevich, "New Religions" and Battle of Ideas, Moskau 1985.
Gordienko, N.S., Sovremennoye russkoye pravoslaviye, Leningrad 1987.

Part 2:

Hoeffing, Helmut, Sibirien - das schlafende Land erwacht, Braunschweig 1985.
Schulz, Alfred, Sibirien-Eine Landeskunde, Breslau 1923.
Stancey, Ton, publ., Bild der Voelker. Die Brockhaus Voelkerkunde Bd. 9: Europa. Asiatische Sowjetunion ohne West Turkenstan, Wiesbaden 1974.
Simon, Gerhard, Russen und Nichtrussen in der UdSSR. Zu den Ergebnissen der Volkszaehlung von 1979. Berichte des Bundesinstitutes fuer ostwissenschaftliche Studien, Koeln II/1981.
Koslov, V.I., Nazionalnosti SSSR, Moskau 1975.
Korsun, E.A., Gosudarstvenni muzey etnografii narodov SSSR, Leningrad 1980.
Tugolukov, W.A., Tungusi (Ewenki i Eweni) w sredniy i zapadnoiy sibiri, Moskva 1985.
Gurvitsch, I.S., Dolgich, B.O., Preobrasovanija w khosyaistve i kulture i etnitsheskiye Prozessi u narodov Severa, Moskau 1970.
Bruk, S.I., Nasseleniye mira. Etnodemografitsheski Slowar, Moskva 1986.
Boikop, Kultura narodov sewera: tradizii i Sovremenasti, Novosibirsk 1986.
Andrijanov, B., Na velikoi russkoi ravnine, Moskva 1984.
Lorimer, F., The population of the Soviet Union, Geneva 1946.
Vallentei, D.I., Demografitisheski enziklopedtitsheski slowar, Moskva 1985.
Dshaoshvili, W.D., Nasselenye Gruzii, Tbilissi 1968.
Volkova, N.G., Kultura i byt narodov severnogo kavkaza (1917-1967), Moskva 1968.
Manedov, K.W., Nasseleniye Aserbaidzhanskoi SSR za 60 Let, Baku 1978.
Kuseyev, P.G., Bashkirskaya SSR za 60 Let sovetskoj vlasti, Ufa 1977.
Rakov, A.A., Nasseleniye BSSR, Minsk 1969.
Vorobyev, W.W., Nasselehiye Vostotshnoi Sibiri, Novosibirsk 1977.
Sergeyeva, K.P., Nasseleniye Dagestana, Machatschkala 1984.
Narodi srednei asii i Kazakhstana, t. 1-2, Moskau 1962.
Pokrovskaya, I.P., Nasseleniye Moldavii, Kishinev 1973.
Kisseleva, G., Problemi rasseleleniya w SSSR, Moskau 1980.

Starikov, W.N., Tatarskaya ASSR, Kasan 1967.

Mulyadshanov, I.R., Narodo-nasseleniye Uzbekskoi SSR, Tashkent 1967.

Sidorov, P.A., Nasseleniye Tashvashii, Tsheboksari 1960 Malij Atlas SSSR, Moskva 1982.

The Soviet Caucasus, Challenge Report 4, Issachar, Seattle 1984.

Shdanko, T.A., Sovietski Soyuz. Respubliki Zakavkazya. Respubliki Srednej Asii Kazakhstan, Moskva 1984.

Karypkulova, A., Kirgiziya, Moskau 1985.

Sufarow, K.A., Uzbekskaya Sovetskaya Sozialistitsheskaya Respublika, Tashkent 1981.

ABOUT THE AUTHOR

Johannes Reimer was born in the Soviet Union and lived there for 21 years. In 1976, he immigrated to West Germany. He has studied theology in West Germany and the U.S. and been a pastor for an evangelical church in West Germany.

Johannes Reimer is the International Director of LOGOS International Biblical Education by Extension which provides Biblical training in Germany, the Soviet Union, and the U.S. Its international headquarters is in Bielefeld, West Germany. He is married to Cornelia Reimer and has one daughter, Stephanie.